UNDERSTAND

Also in this series:

COLOUR THERAPY
Mary Anderson
HOW TO BE A MEDIUM
J. Donald Walters
HOW TO DEVELOP YOUR ESP
Zak Martin
MEDITATION: THE INNER WAY
Naomi Humphrey
PRACTICAL VISUALIZATION
Chris Odle
UNDERSTANDING ASTRAL PROJECTION
Anthony Martin
UNDERSTANDING THE CHAKRAS
Peter Rendel
UNDERSTANDING THE I CHING
Tom Riseman
UNDERSTANDING NUMEROLOGY
D. Jason Cooper
UNDERSTANDING PALMISTRY
Mary Anderson
UNDERSTANDING REINCARNATION
J. H. Brennan

UNDERSTANDING RUNES

Their origins and magical power

by

Michael Howard

THE AQUARIAN PRESS

This edition 1990
First published as *The Magic of the Runes* 1980

British Library Cataloguing in Publication Data

Howard, Michael
Understanding runes: their origins and magical power.
(Aquarian paths to inner power).
1. Runes. Occult aspects
I. Title
133. 33

ISBN 1-85538-013-7

*The Aquarian Press is part of the Thorsons Publishing Group,
Wellingborough, Northamptonshire NN8 2RQ, England*

Printed in Great Britain by William Collins, Sons & Co. Ltd,
Glasgow

1 3 5 7 9 10 8 6 4 2

CONTENTS

CHAPTER ONE

THE ORIGINS OF THE RUNES

The Norse and Saxon runic alphabet is an ancient form of writing which is shrouded in historical and occult mystery. Very little is known of its magical uses although rune magic was widely practised for many hundreds of years. What scant information that is available has to be gleaned from obscure historical records, research into ancient religious practices, the surviving traditions of popular folklore and the weathered inscriptions on pagan and semi-Christian standing stones.

Definitions of the word 'rune' are many and varied. It can be traced back to the Old Nordic and Anglo-Saxon *run*, early Icelandic *runar* and Old German *runa*. These in turn are derived from the Indo-European root word *ru*, which means alternatively 'mystery' or 'secret', and the Old High German *runer*, usually translated as 'whisper'. The slang term to rown, roon or round in the ear was widely used in Anglo-Saxon England to refer to the whispering of a secret and is obviously derived from rune.

From this popular usage (which is a good indication of sacred or taboo subjects transformed into common everyday situations) we can discern that the runes were a secret or semi-secret alphabet used by initiates of the occult and pagan traditions to pass on magical information. They originated in the prehistoric rock carvings known as the Hallristinger script which were made by Neolithic and Bronze Age tribes who settled in northern Italy. There is a distinct similarity between the runic alphabet and the old Etruscan forms of writing which seems to support the theory of a north Italian origin. The unusual angular strokes of the runes are probably due to the fact that they were originally hewn into stone. Such actions would prohibit the use of curves and rounded letters in the alphabet.

Odin — the God of the Runes

Mythologically, the invention of the runes is credited to the Nordic god Odin. His name is said to be derived from the Old Norse word *Od*, meaning 'wind' or 'spirit'. The Roman historian and traveller Tacitus identified Odin or Woden (as he was sometimes called by German pagans) with Mercury, the Roman god who invented writing. The physical description of Odin indicates his sinister reputation. He is usually depicted as a tall, thin man wearing a long cloak and with grey hair falling in tangled locks to his shoulders. Odin's face is strong and hard, he has only one eye which stares into the distance and burns blue. His gaping eye socket is hidden by a wide-brimmed, soft hat pulled down over one side of his face. He leans on a blackthorn staff and is accompanied by a raven and a wolf.

Odin has the power to raise the dead, divine the future, fly through the sky on his eight-legged horse and change his shape at will. Travellers would often meet the god as he wandered the bleak winter landscape in human form. The

Danish king Harald Wartooth met him and the old god promised the monarch immunity from wounds in battle. In return King Harald pledged all the souls which his sword drove from their bodies to Odin. However, when the king betrayed Odin the god materialized at a battle in the shape of his enemy and slew him. It seems that Odin cannot be trusted to keep a pact.

Sometimes Odin is referred to by the name *Grim*. This is an Old English term meaning 'hooded' or 'masked'. It survives in the name *Grimsdyke* which is an ancient dyke at Harrow Weald, Middlesex, obviously dedicated to the god. Interestingly, the Celts possessed a divine hierarchy of hooded gods known as the *Genii Cucullati* or Hooded Ones. A stone plaque depicting three of these deities was unearthed at Houseteads in Northumberland and dates from the third century CE (Common Era). Little is known of these gods except that they were associated with some kind of magical horse cult. This may be tenuously linked with the runes through the occult activities of the Fraternity of Horse Whisperers who still survive in rural parts of East Anglia and the West Country. They claim to be able to tame wild horses by whispering magical incantations and seem to have originated in some pre-Christian religious cult which venerated the horse goddess. Although it is speculation, there may be a link here between Odin the hooded god, the Celtic *Genii Cucullati* and a pagan horse cult that used runes for magical purposes.

It is said that Odin gained his secret knowledge of the runes by a supreme act of self-sacrifice. He hung for nine days and nights impaled by his own spear to the Yggdrasil or World Tree to gain this forbidden wisdom. Nine is, of course, a lunar number representing the three phases of the moon (i.e. waxing, full and waning) multiplied by itself. In pagan mythology the moon is a symbol of inspiration, psychic power and the feminine aspect of Nature represented by the ever-fertile Earth Mother image. It is also said that Odin had drunk deeply from the sacred mead in the cauldron of inspiration, owned by the god Mimer to learn the mysteries of life and death. The price he paid for this knowledge was the loss of an eye. The cauldron is an ancient symbol of the Great Mother Goddess and in these myths we can discern the relics of the old moon worship and earth magic which was slowly becoming subservient to the new patriarchy of the male gods.

The Secret of the Shamans

The possibility exists, and it is a strong one, that Odin may have been a historical personage who was deified after his death. This is a common theme in mythological history and some religious experts believe that the legends of such gods as Isis, Osiris, Bran and Bridget may be based on the lives of real people who civilized their respective countries and were worshipped as divine beings after they had passed on.

If this theory is tenable in the case of Odin then he may possibly have been a prehistoric shaman who discovered a magical alphabet after a ritual of self-sacrifice. Shamanism was the primitive (and I do not use the word in any derogatory way) religion of many parts of pre-Christian Europe and the shaman became a powerful figure in the tribal community and was both feared and respected. In anthropological terms the shaman is a man or woman with the psychic ability to contact the spirit world and communicate with its inhabitants. This was usually achieved while the shaman was in a trance-like state induced by drugs, ritual, dancing or fasting. The shaman also possessed the ability to divine the future, was able to find missing objects or persons by clairvoyant powers and could speak to the dead.

The shaman is 'different' from other people in a way which it is hard for we in the West, who have lost contact with the natural forces of our planet, to understand. Within his or her cultural situation the shaman is a unique person. They are feared because of their great powers for good and evil yet command the respect of those who depend on them. It is the shaman who protects the tribal community from its enemies (human or animal), ensures by magic a good harvest, knows the occult properties of herbs for healing the sick, can perceive the changing pattern of the future and, as his or her last gift to the dependent tribe, selects a replacement who will become the next shaman in line.

Shamanism still exists in many parts of the world and can be found in remote areas of Siberia (where even Communism has failed to destroy the old beliefs of the ethnic people who inhabit that icy region), in the East Indies, North and South America, Africa and Australia. Practitioners of the shamanistic tradition can even still be found in the country districts of 'civilized' Europe where the pagan religion survives under a thin veneer of token Christianity. In all cases the shaman can be recognized by his or her 'differentness' and the self-imposed isolation from the community required in order to obtain the powers to help it. The world of the shaman is so different from our own that we would have to experience something of it before we could fully understand its *modus operandi*. The shaman's universe is completely magical. Nothing is simply ordinary, nowhere are things exactly what they seem. His world has no place for the single vision which the poet William Blake said was the lack of imaginative response in Western European culture. Everything has magical significance to the shaman. He or she has learnt to read the signs and omens placed by the Earth Mother in the natural world to guide Her children and, by gaining this knowledge can, in turn, help those of us who lack this sublime vision of creation.

Shamanistic Vision

It is almost impossible to convey the magical awareness which the shaman possesses as a natural quality to Westerners who have broken the umbilical cord to Mother Earth. In our times, matters of the spirit have either been relegated to an occasional trip to the local Christian church for a wedding, baptism or funeral or have become the focus of outdated superstitions based on an irrational fear of the unknown. We have wrapped ourselves up in a technological cocoon and from its warm, cosy security make two-fingered gestures of derision at the old, shamanistic beliefs which were the origins of our present day religious impulses. In fact although the shaman may not be 'educated' in the way that the average person in the West understands that word (i.e. conditioned from childhood to accept a materialistic, single vision of the cosmic pattern) his or her awareness of the natural environment in which we live, breath, sleep and eventually die is a million times more concentrated and potent than the narrow image of the world which we experience through senses dulled and blurred by our unmagical civilization.

Just by walking down a woodland path, observing the texture and roundness of a stone, the colour of a dead leaf curled embryo-like on the earth, listening to the cries of the birds in the trees, feeling the elemental power of the wind or scrying the tracks of animals in the fresh snow, the shaman can tune in to the subtle vibrations of that state of being which exists in the nether regions between the worlds of matter and the realms of spirit. Such perception is a rare ability in our modern society but it is the treasured possession of a few rare individuals who understand and share the shamanistic view of life. These chosen few include among their ranks artists, poets, writers and mystics who can achieve the Oneness with the forces of Nature which is the mark of the true shaman and single him or her out from the rest of humanity.

Gateway to Occult Knowledge

How does the shaman gain this experience? There are various methods used to attain the special trance state which allows contact with the spiritual side of nature. These include the use by shamans of natural psychedelic agents such as the hallucination-inducing 'sacred mushroom'. This is known by its Latin name as *amanita muscaria*. Other, safer, methods of inducing trance are by breathing exercises, yoga techniques, sensory deprivation, fasting and ritual dance. There are also more hazardous methods such as flagellation, ritual sex and self-torture which were (and indeed still are) practised by the North American Indian shamans. If we return to the Norse legend of the hooded god Odin we find that he was impaled for nine days and nights by his own spear. At the end of this experience he achieved the vision of the magical runic alphabet. Similar rituals are known to the native Americans. Young braves are suspended by hooks dug deep into their flesh from the eaves of the medicine lodges. Pain is regarded by some priests of the native religions (rightly or wrongly) as a tool to open up the psychic centres of the body which, in Eastern mysticism, are termed the *chakras*.

Sacrificial Rites

In my previous book *The Runes and other Magical Alphabets* (The Aquarian Press, Wellingborough, 1981), I mentioned the rites of initiation into the Odinic Mysteries. I speculated that these ceremonies included a symbolic sacrifice of the initiate by hanging him on a yew tree. Such a ritual gesture may have been a copy of the original act by which the god received the runic lore. At a later period this symbolic rite became debased and was interpreted in a more literal and horrific way as human sacrifice. This practice seems to have developed from the funeral rites of stabbing corpses with spears and then burning them, which was apparently an Odinist custom. However, a Christian abbot writing in the eleventh century CE gives a graphic description of the bodies of sacrificed men and animals hanging from trees around a temple to Odin at Uppsala in Sweden. Giving the good abbot the benefit of the doubt (Christian chroniclers of pagan rites were well known for their ability to distort the facts and exaggerate the 'nasty' aspects of the old beliefs, which they detested), it seems that such practices were performed at the temple at special festivals held every nine years to commemorate the death of the hooded god of the runes. Is it possible that the past appetite in this country for public hangings and the strong feelings at present flowing through the land to restore capital punishment may be an unconscious racial memory of these debased and cruel rites to Odin? In the world of magic anything is possible and the old cliché that truth is stranger than fiction is often perfectly correct.

Odin the Man

Support for the belief that Odin may have been a real

person is offered by Robert Macoy. He claims that Odin was originally the chieftain of an Asiatic tribe who emigrated from his homeland, travelled across Central Europe and settled finally in Scandinavia. There he established a kingdom, formulated new laws and established a mystery religion. He assumed the magic name of Odin and founded a priesthood of 12 wise men (representative of the zodiacal signs) who administered the kingdom, celebrated the religious ceremonies and acted as prophets, divining the future for the benefit of the local people.

According to the American esoteric philosopher Manly Palmer Hall, writing in his epic masterpiece *The Secret Teachings of All Ages* (Philosophical Research Society) this historical Odin was mythologized after his death and identified with a local god of the same name. This is a similar process to the deification of the historical Jesus of Nazareth, who, it would seem, was a Jewish rabbi with extraordinary psychic powers. After his crucifixion he was accepted by a minor group of Zionist extremists as the Messiah promised by the Old Testament prophecies. In pagan history, as we noted before, respected administrators who acted as civilizers in periods of national stress were often conferred with posthumous godships by their grateful public. Today famous movie stars such as Rudolph Valentino, James Dean and Marilyn Monroe have nearly attained the same divine status in the eyes of their adoring fans.

The Odinic Mysteries

Manly Palmer Hall states that the sacred mysteries of Odin were celebrated in nine (again note the mystical lunar number associated with the old moon worshippers) caves which symbolically represented the nine ascending worlds of spirit. The candidate for initiation into the Mysteries symbolized Odin's son Baldur who was murdered by the trickery of Loki, in an action-replay of the legend of the murder of the sun god Osiris by his brother/son Set in Ancient Egyptian mythology. Each cave that the initiate travelled through during the long and arduous ceremony also represented one of the spheres of nature. The priests who conducted the initiation ritual were symbols of the sun, the moon and the stars and also represented the planetary spirits associated with these heavenly bodies in northern myths.

The candidate eventually emerged from the last cave in the symbolic journey through the spirit worlds into a sacred inner sanctum that had a roof lined with battle shields. In this holy chamber the initiate took an oath of secrecy and a vow of allegiance to Odin. Finally, in recognition of the god, the initiate kissed the naked blade of a war sword. He then drank the special mead, laced with aromatic herbs, from a bowl made from a human skull. He was presented with a silver ring engraved with runic characters and told that he had passed through the gates of death and had been reborn as a perfected being.

If Manly Palmer Hall's account of the Odinic Mysteries can be accepted as fact, and there is little reason to doubt the authenticity of his research into ancient religious practices, the initiate not only represented Baldur but came face to face with an effigy of the god at the end of his journey through the nine worlds. This is a magico-religious practice which was well known in pagan initiatory rituals. In those involving a ceremonial maze when the neophyte reached the centre, he or she faced a bronze mirror reflecting back their own image. This was a way of teaching the initiate the meaning of the words engraved over the gate of the Delphic oracle — 'Know Thyself' — and also taught the lesson that the real spiritual truth cannot be found outside but must be experienced within.

Manly Hall states quite categorically that the burial mound of King Odin is said to be situated near the old god's major shrine at Uppsala in Sweden. We do not know if this folk legend has ever been verified by archaeological survey of the mound to see if a great chieftain is buried there. Despite this lack of verification it does provide further evidence that, in popular belief, Odin was regarded as a historical person who later became regarded as a divine being.

The Cult of Kingship

As Dr William Chaney states in his *Cult of Kingship in Anglo-Saxon England* (Manchester University Press) almost every Anglo-Saxon Royal House claimed descent from their divine ancestor Woden or Odin. This allegiance to the old god — or rather his original, human representative, the ancient shaman priest-king — was brought to England by the invading Germanic tribes. Significantly, according to Dr Chaney, this belief survived the conversion of the Saxons to Christianity.

In Germanic and Scandinavian mythology and tribal society the king was the high priest of the Odinic Mysteries and was called, in Norse poetry, 'the warden of the holy temple of Odin'. In accordance with this belief the Royal Houses of the Anglo-Saxons were regarded as hereditary divine families descended from the high god Woden. It is therefore logical to assume that these rulers claimed lineal descent, either literally or symbolically, from the first tribal king who assumed the name Odin. He was the priest-king who received the sacred runic alphabet by means of a shamanistic rite of self-sacrifice.

Dr Chaney points out that the prefix *Os*, signifying 'heathen god' or 'divine', occurs in no less than 12 names of ancient Northumbrian kings. All but two of these died violently, leading some folklore experts to suggest that they were sacrificial victims in the dark traditions of pagan Odinism. Dr Chaney regards the word *Os* to be reminiscent of the spirits of the North Wind in Norse mythology and further states that it is a common term used by Icelanders to describe their pre-Christian deities.

Os is also mentioned in a Saxon rune poem of the eighth or ninth century CE and is referred to as '... the beginning of every speech'. Dr Chaney says this refers to Odin who was the god that gave the magical words (i.e. the runes) that began every important statement or speech in Norse or Germanic tribal gatherings. Therefore we seem to have here a firm connection between the god Odin, the inventor of runes, the spirits of the North Wind, the Northumberland royal dynasty and the pagan belief in divine kingship.

Woden worship is said by Dr Chaney to have originated in the Rhineland or the south-east area of Europe. It was only later in history that the cult of the hooded rune god entered northern Europe, carried by the migrating tribes of Indo-European peoples who were its devotees. This supports the theory of Robert Macoy who postulates an Asian warrior king who, migrating northwards from his tribal homelands, established a divine kingdom in Scandinavia, based on sacrificial ceremonies, magical alphabets and shamanism.

CHAPTER TWO

THE RUNE
MASTERS

Before examining the magical qualities of the runic alphabet it would be prudent to discover a little more about the people who used the runes and especially about those chosen few who claimed to be adepts in ancient rune magic.

The wizards who used the runes for magical purposes regarded themselves as blood kin to Odin, the Nordic god who was popularly accredited with inventing the runic alphabet. As we have seen, they were basically followers of the shamanistic tradition which is one of the oldest, if not the oldest, religious belief system known to humanity. These beliefs dated back to the early Stone Age people and their simplistic, yet essential, concept of the life force which they symbolized in art and ritual as a male Horned God and a female Moon Goddess or Earth Mother.

According to the Scottish occultist and writer Lewis Spence the term *shaman* is derived from a Manchurian word meaning 'one who is excited'. This is a direct reference to the state of near hysteria cultivated by the shaman in order to communicate with the spirits of the departed and the elemental inhabitants of the mystical Otherworld that exists beyond the material senses. A shaman can, in theory, be of any religion yet is of none for he or she (the term is a neutral one without gender, like witch) is a disciple of the oldest religion practised by humanity.

Shamanistic Training

Shamanism, like hereditary witchcraft, is passed down in families from generation to generation. It is usually transmitted from mother to daughter and father to son. When a person decides to take up the shaman's cloak he or she retires into the forest or tundra for three days to prepare for the traumatic experience of initiation. During this period the shaman lives in harmony with nature and refuses to partake of food or drink. During this period of enforced isolation the novice receives his or her mediumistic powers (the ability to speak with spirits) through the magical action of some natural object. This object may be a stone, a tree or an animal which becomes a ritual totem or power source for the shaman when he or she returns to the tribe.

The psychic training of a shaman lasts for two to three years at the minimum. It consists of occult exercises designed to open up the psychic centres in the body and allow contact with the guardian spirits of the Otherworld. Physical training, which is just as arduous as the controlling of the psychic side of the shaman's abilities, consists of instructions by the elders of the tribe in the ritual and seasonal dances, magical songs and the use of the special spirit drum which is used by the shaman to make contact with the Otherworld.

The spirit drum was the most important magical instrument used in the shamanistic ceremonies. It was similar to the traditional Irish or Scottish bodhrann drum which today is a feature of many folk music groups. It is very basically constructed from a wooden hoop over which is stretched tight animal hide or a piece of vellum. This is fixed in place by brass tacks to form a completely rigid playing surface. No iron can be used in the construction of this drum for it is an old belief that this metal negates the power raised in magical rites. Shamanistic spirit drums had occult symbols or demon faces painted on their surfaces and runic characters etched around the rim. The drum could be played either with the flat of the hand or by using a double-headed drumstick carved from wood or bone.

Shamans often received instructions and occult teachings through dreams, which in many cases were like visions. In these dreams the spirits of the Otherworld materialized in the shape of animals and spoke to them. Such experiences are a common feature of magical initiation especially in ethnic societies. Recently, psychologists such as Dr Carl Jung have carefully researched the hidden symbolism of dreams and have discovered that they are an important aspect of personal development. Whether we remember them or not every person dreams and those dreams which are in colour or spring easily to our conscious mind when we awake are important and should be analysed carefully. In dreams the subconscious yields its many secrets and we can contact the archetypal images which lurk in the racial memory of all of us. We can indeed become our own shamans.

Shamanistic Initiation

An important part of the shamanistic initiation rituals was

the ceremony known as the 'Ascent of the Tree'. This involved the setting up of a birch pole in a forest clearing. A goat or some other small animal was sacrificed and its blood smeared on the nine openings of the shaman's naked body to seal them from invasion by negative forces. The master shaman then climbed the pole, cutting nine notches in it as he went. The initiate then followed the master shaman up the birch pole in a journey which was symbolic of the soul's ascension through the nine worlds of heaven. The birch pole used in this ceremony represents the pillar or sacred tree which stands at the centre of the world and points up at the North Star which is the realm of the old gods. This sacred tree connects the material world of the senses with the spiritual sphere of the psyche. When the shaman listens to the hypnotic beat of the spirit drum he astrally projects his soul to the World Tree (the Yggdrasil in Norse mythology) which is the ladder of ascension to the spirit kingdom.

As soon as the shaman has passed all the tests set by his master and completed his psychic and physical training a special ceremony takes place during which the new recruit is formally accepted as a full-blooded wizard. He is led to the top of a hill dressed in ceremonial regalia which will include the pelts of several sacred animals. He is handed a magic rattle and told to repeat a vow of fidelity to the matters of the spirit and renounces all worldly things. The final initiation of the new shaman comes when he is given his familiar spirits who will remain with him until his death, when they vanish. A similar tradition is recorded in the accounts of traditional witches in rural England.

Often the initiation rituals include, as do so many pagan rituals, a symbolic act of death and rebirth. In the ceremonies of certain Eskimo shamans the neophyte remains for many hours meditating in an igloo. After a period of time has lapsed he becomes unconscious and remains in a state of coma for three days. During this self-imposed trance he experiences intense visions which include meetings with shadowy demons from the underworld and being eaten alive by a giant polar bear. Eventually the shaman regains consciousness and, in the terminology of psycho-magical experience, is reborn as a new personality. While in the trance he has been cleansed of his past errors and defects in character and emerges from the icy womb of the igloo as an enlightened being.

Among the tribal communities of northern Siberia, Finland and Lapland the shaman combined the role of medicine man, priest and prophet. He was also the medium used by the tribe to make contact with the spirits of the dead and predict the future. In the case of the latter he may well have used the runes for divination. Alternatively, he would have employed the spirit drum, using its steady beat to fall into a trance during which prophecies would be uttered and advice given. Sometimes the shaman spoke in strange languages or unknown dialects. Often he would become possessed by spirits and some of these would try to bring harm to the shaman and those gathered around his entranced body.

The Regalia of the Rune Masters

Shamans were the spiritual descendants of the sorcerers and priest-magicians of the Stone and Bronze Ages. Some of the remains of these practitioners of the occult arts have been discovered, almost perfectly preserved, in the peat bogs of Denmark. One of these burials was unearthed at Lyngby near Copenhagen at the end of the nineteenth century. Archaeologists excavating the site discovered the remains of an oak coffin which contained the skeleton of a man who had obviously been a shaman.

In the coffin was a leather bag containing amber heads (which in neolithic times had a magical significance which survives to this day in folklore), a conch shell (a fertility symbol which was a thinly disguised representation of the female sexual organs), a falcon's claw (possibly a hunting amulet or magic charm granting the power to fly), the bones of a snake (traditionally associated with healing), a squirrel's tail and the dried entrails of a small rodent.

The archaeologists who examined this find believed they had stumbled on the burial place of a local priest-magician. Confirmation came when they found a forked hazel twig in the coffin wrapped in animal skin. This they identified as a magical wand or sceptre of office carried by the ancient shaman as a token of his power.

In fact the shamans and rune masters of Northern Europe were easily distinguished from ordinary people by the distinctive regalia which denoted their special calling. They wore ritual head-dresses made from the fur of woodland creatures such as the badger and the fox, a woollen cloak dyed blue — one of the sacred colours of the Norse god Odin — and carried a leather pouch filled with dried herbs and charms. As a mark of their trade the rune masters carried a special staff or baton made of ash or hazel wood which was carved with runic sigils.

Unusual costumes worn by high-ranking initiates were also known in the annals of European witchcraft which was a debased form of the old animistic religion followed by shaman priests. A seventeenth century portrait of a male witch, described by witchcraft writer Dr Margaret Murray in one of her articles for the journal of the Folklore Society, provides us with an eye-witness description which supports this notion. The portrait depicts a moon-faced man clad in a faery-green hood with bells like a jester's cap and a russet-coloured jerkin. He holds in his strong hands a brindle cat which is obviously supposed to be his familiar.

Writing in 1584 Reginald Scot, author of *The Discoverie of Witchcraft*, mentioned a kind of uniform worn by prominent witches. Such magical attire seems to have survived even today. In 1946 it was reliably reported that East Anglian witches possessed a ceremonial costume which was passed down from generation to generation. It consisted of three weasel, stoat or polecat skins worn around the neck and hanging down between the breasts like a kind of ritual collar. Special decorations of this type were apparently sported by Suffolk witches in the pre-war years.

In *The Saga of Erik the Red* an anonymous author writing in the late thirteenth century CE provides us with an interesting description of a rune mistress:

> She wore a cloak set with stones along the hem.
> Around her neck and covering her head [was] a hood
> of white catskin. In one hand she carried a staff with a
> knob at the end. At her belt, holding her dress
> together, was a charm pouch. She wore catskin shoes
> and mittens to cover her hands.

An Icelandic seeress and runecaster describes her magical talents in the following folk song:

> Hedi, me call me when their homes I visit.
> A far seeing witch, wise in talismans,
> Caster of spells, cunning in magic,
> To wicked women welcome always.
>
> Arm rings and necklaces Odin ye gave me,
> To learn my lore, to learn all magics,
> Wider and wider, through all worlds I see.

Outside I sat myself when ye came,
Terror of the gods and gazed in my eyes,
What do ye ask of me?
Why tempt me?

Odin! O know ye, I know where they lost eye has gone,
Hidden deep in Mimir's well,
Mimir each man's mead he drinks,
Well, would ye know more.

The reference in the second verse to the arm rings and
necklaces given to the witch by the hooded god may refer
to magical bracelets and pendants which were marks of her
status in the tribe. In the third verse, first line, she refers to
astral travel. This is the occult technique of projecting the
spirit from the physical body at will. It was a skill practised
by the northern shamans and the secret knowledge of its
practice was inherited by later rune masters and mistresses.

Runic Skill

Incorrect use of a rune could spell deadly danger for the
magician or witch. The old rune masters believed that every
rune was associated with an elemental spirit or force which
had to be carefully evoked and once conjured into physical
form had to be very carefully controlled. If this entity
escaped the magician then it would be unleashed on an
unsuspecting world and create havoc. Some of the spirits
evoked by the shamans were believed by them to be
succubi and incubi. These were lustful earth spirits who
delighted in sexual relations with humans in the shape of
beautiful women or handsome young boys. Their carnal
appetites were insatiable and any person who became

possessed by them could be literally fornicated to death.

There was also the real danger that people who had not received the proper occult training in runecraft could dabble with them and both hurt themselves and others. For instance, the use of a cursing rune when a healing one was required would have dire results for both the patient and the would-be rune master who would have to face the vengeance of the victim's relatives.

One famous rune master named Egill was called to a house where a woman laying dying from a fever. A rival rune master had already been called in to minister to the sick woman but despite his assistance she hovered on the brink of death. Egill immediately identified the source of the trouble. His rival had scored the wrong runes on a fragment of whale bone hanging above the patient's bed. Angrily, Egill denounced the quack runecasters who claimed to be skilled in runic magic yet lacked the knowledge to apply runic lore correctly:

> Runes shall not a man score,
> save he can read them well,
> that many a man betideth on a
> mirk stave to stumble,
> saw I on a scraped whale bone
> ten dark staves scored
> thou hath to the leek widen
> over long sickness broughton.

The skilled rune master immediately erased the incorrect runes on the bone and replaced them with his own runic healing charm. This he placed under the sick woman's pillow and within a few minutes she was restored to full health once more.

Egill was very well versed in the secrets of the runes. Once he narrowly escaped death at the hands of an assassin, hired by a rival magician, by using the runes. He carved runes around the rim of a drinking cup which he suspected had been poisoned by his enemy. These he reddened with his own blood and immediately the drinking horn shattered into fragments and its tainted contents were spilt on the floor. If the drink had not been poisoned the runes would not have broken the cup.

CHAPTER THREE

THE RUNIC SCRIPTS

The different types of runic alphabet and their use, either together or intermixed, make it extremely difficult for students of the runes to trace their origins with any degree of accuracy. There are Germanic runes, Old English or Anglo-Saxon runes, Scandinavian (Norwegian, Swedish and Danish) runes and Gothic runes. During the Romantic period of the eighteenth century, when rich aristocrats dabbled in the occult, the invention of pseudo-runic alphabets became a popular pastime. Some inscriptions may still survive featuring these phoney runes and they add one more problem for the researcher who is seeking reliable information on runic history.

The Symbolic Meanings of the Runic Script

For ease of use I have rationalized the Norse and Germanic

runes into a composite alphabet. In the Middle Ages the runes were translated into the letters of the Latin alphabet by monkish chroniclers and were used as an ordinary alphabet. But by this time their pagan lore and magical symbolism had largely been debased or lost. The real spiritual significance and mystical power of the runes came from the symbolic meanings attributed to each of the characters by the rune wizards and the shamans of the northern European version of the pagan Old Religion. These esoteric meanings are given below for each rune, together with the Old English magical title and popular descriptive name. Their magico-spiritual symbolism reflects their divinatory meaning, which will be described in Chapter Seven.

FEOH   In ancient times this rune signified cattle,
                  which were commonly used as a form of hard
                  currency among the Indo-European tribes. This
                  rune therefore represents wealth, but as
Frey   cattle raids between the warring tribes were
                  frequent, it is wealth which can be easily won
                  or lost.

In Norse mythology the Feoh rune was sacred to the deity known as Frey. He is the ithyphallic god of fertility, peace and happiness. Frey belonged to the elder dynasty of Norse gods known as the Vanir. These deities have an ancient lineage and were the original gods and goddesses worshipped in northern Europe during the Bronze Age.

Frey's magical totem animals are the boar and the horse. Archaeologists have uncovered helmets and ceremonial masks in the form of a boar's face from Viking burial sites. This symbol of Frey survives in the Yuletide tradition of the boar's head which was carried into medieval banquets on a silver platter garlanded with herbs and apples.

UR

Π

Power

This rune symbolizes the auroch or wild ox, an ancient breed of European bison dating back to prehistoric times. The Ur rune is a symbol of elemental power and masculine energy in its untamed form. The ritual hunting of the auroch was undertaken by young warriors as a test of manhood. Therefore Ur can be seen as representing the pioneer spirit, rugged individualism and spiritual strength.

In pagan Europe beasts such as bulls, rams, goats, stags and bison were sacred to the Horned God whose image first appears in Stone Age cave paintings. Later versions of the Horned One such as Cernnunos and Herne are familiar as sacred icons in Celtic and Saxon mythology. Esoterically, the Horned God was the Lord of the Animals in the wildwood and acted as a messenger between Midgard, or Middle Earth, and the Otherworld.

PORN

▷

Thor

This runic character represents a thorn but also the magical hammer of the god Thor which is called Mjollnir. Although a thorn is only tiny in size it can still cause physical discomfort which is increased a hundredfold if thorns are encountered in large numbers.

In some of the medieval sources the name of this rune is translated as 'giant' or 'demon'. This was a later Christian reference to the thunder god Thor who was regarded as an evil entity. When the new religion came to Europe the pagan gods of the Old Faith were transformed into demons in Christian propaganda and their adherents were described as devil worshippers.

It is interesting that the shamans and traditional witches in olden times used a blackthorn staff or wand for magical workings. These objects allegedly had the power to direct curses and could blast the souls of their enemies. On a magical level this rune represents the traditional ability of the rune wizard to conjure up elemental forces and the powers of chaos.

OS

Odin

Often known as 'the divine rune', Os is sacred to Odin the Allfather as the Supreme Being of Norse pagan religion in its historical period. Odin was regarded by the Romans as the northern European equivalent of Mercury or Hermes. This rune is therefore associated with communication through the written and spoken word.

The Os rune is a symbol of the arcane wisdom imparted to human beings from divine sources through clairvoyance or magical vision. It is also related to the bardic teachings which were an important aspect of the Indo-European shamanic tradition. Odin was the god of storms and it was often thought that his divine messages could be heard in the howling winds at midwinter which accompanied the Wild Hunt.

RAD

Wheel

In rune lore this character was associated with the symbol of a wheel or wagon. The latter was a recurring motif in Norse myth and could be either the chariot of the sun which crosses the sky every day, the magical vehicles which transported Freyja and Frey, Thor's chariot drawn by two giant goats or the sacred wagon of the earth goddess Nerthus.

These symbols are very ancient ones and predate the Vikings by 1,000 years. Effigies of horses drawing a primitive wagon on which the sun rests have been excavated in Scandinavia and date from the early Bronze Age. In the shamanic tradition these magical vehicles carry the initiate from the mortal world of Middle Earth and through the veil of the unseen to the divine realm of the Old Gods.

CEN

<

Fire

This is a rune symbolizing the elemental power of fire. A torch or sacred fire is a universal symbol of enlightenment found in most religions. In Nordic mythology the two primal forces responsible for creation, which brought the physical universe into manifestation, are fire (masculine energy) and ice (feminine energy).

The Cen rune is associated with those of noble birth who were often initiated into the pagan Mysteries. The role of priest-king or priestess-queen is a common feature of pagan religion both in Europe and the Middle East. Cen was also linked with ritual burning of sacred fires on hill-tops in pre-Christian times to celebrate the solstices at midwinter and midsummer and the spring and autumn equinoxes.

GYFU

X

Gift

In tribal society the giving of gifts had a very special significance. A wealthy person was judged by the number and frequency of the gifts he or she gave to those less fortunate. Personal relationships and close friendships were also cemented by the exchanging of gifts which were of small value but had a considerable symbolic meaning.

'A gift offered to the gods' was also a polite euphemism for sacrificial offerings. These could be in the form of food, jewellery, coins or the blood sacrifice of an animal or human being. This practice is an aspect of pagan religious belief which is difficult to defend from a moral standpoint. However, we should resist any attempt to be smug about it when modern society still possesses the slaughter of the abattoir, the obscene horrors of the vivisection laboratory and the waste of young men sacrificed to the gods of war.

In the Viking Age the candidates for human sacrifice were criminals found guilty of capital offences or prisoners-of-war. These unfortunates were often sacrificed to Odin and the approved form of execution was by hanging or garroting with a leather thong. This was an ancient practice which predated the Vikings. Bronze Age burials of mummified bodies found in Danish peat-bogs have been identified by archaeologists as sacrificial victims whose lives were dedicated to the Great Mother Goddess. The Celtic Druids also practised this form of sacrifice and one of their victims was recently unearthed from a marsh at Lindow in Cheshire.

WYN

ᚹ

Joy

The meaning of this rune is usually rendered as 'joy' or 'happiness', which were highlights in the lives of the inhabitants of the cold and dark northern regions. Especially near the Arctic Circle, the winters were long and darkness lasted most of the day. The coming of spring was therefore a joyous event celebrated with the worship of the life force.

Some authorities have linked the Wyn rune with the Germanic version of Odin who was called Wotan or Woden. He was later confused with the Christian St Nicholas and became Santa Claus, who brings joy and happiness to children on Christmas Eve. In Germanic myth

Woden, in common with his Nordic counterpart, [...]
leader of the spooky Wild Hunt which rides thro[...]
midwinter sky collecting the souls of the dead.

HAGEL   Translated this rune's name means 'hail', and it
            symbolizes the unexpected spring storms
            which could devastate the germinating crops.
            Hagel therefore represents the delays and
Air   limitations which can often hinder progress,
            either in daily life or on the spiritual path.
            These delays had to be seen in a positive light
            as part of the natural pattern.

While the Norse religion, like all pagan belief systems, was terracentric and worshipped Nature as the manifestation of spiritual forces, the northern European shamans knew that the elements could be disruptive. They fully understood that Nature was not always benevolent but could easily be 'red in tooth and claw'. The modern tendency to sentimentalize the natural world did not exist in ancient times.

Although the Norse people had no real concept of an infernal underworld before the arrival of the Christian missionaries they did recognize a realm of the dead which was ruled over by the dark goddess Hel. The name of the Christian underworld where wicked souls suffer eternal damnation was derived from this deity. This concept of hell would have been unknown to the Nordic pagans. However, the shaman did attempt to mediate the destructive powers of the goddess Hel by evoking the frost giants who represented the hostile elemental forces of winter. They would also have invoked Heimdall, the 'white god' who was the guardian of the Rainbow Bridge between Asgard and Middle Earth and was associated with the Hagel rune.

NYD

Ⴣ

Need

Often modern runecasters use a blank rune to signify Wyrd or 'destiny'. Alternatively, this rune can be used as a substitute. Nyd is ruled by the Norns who, as we shall see in a later chapter, were goddesses who personified the cosmic powers of destiny and fate. It is the Norns who record the deeds of mortals on the scroll of eternity.

Attempts have been made to compare the Norse concept of Wyrd with the belief in karma which is found in Eastern religions and has permeated esotericism in the West. In karmic philosophy it is taught that the positive and negative acts carried out by an individual in this life have to be balanced, either now or in some future incarnation. The Wyrd has some attributes which are similar to this idea of karmic debt but it is more inclined towards the concept of a personal destiny or fate which cannot be avoided and is mapped out for the incarnating soul at birth. The distinction between karma and the Wyrd is a subtle but very important one.

IS

|

Ice

This is the second primal rune, the opposite to Cen. It represents the elemental power of water (spirit) which is transformed into ice (matter) to create physical reality. In the Norse creation myth it was the primordial interaction between fire and ice which triggered this process and manifested Middle Earth.

With the coming of Christianity to the northern lands, the conflict of fire and ice to create the universe was misinterpreted as a dualistic struggle between light and darkness. As with all the polarities which are found in the material world, fire and ice have to be opposing forces. However they also have the potential to unite and create the harmony which is life.

In poetic terms Is is described as 'cold and slippery/it glistens bright as glass like a gem/the field covered with frost is beautiful to see'. This description indicates that the rune is a vision of Nature in her cold and yet beautiful form. The winter wonderland of the north, with its deep snow and icicles hanging from every fir tree, was regarded by the people who lived there as both a hostile and a beautiful environment. They knew, however, that the snows would melt in the spring and the cycle of life would begin again.

GER

Earth

The Ger rune is a symbol of growth, rebirth, regeneration and the harvest which ends the agricultural year. Its form represents the wheel or cycle of the seasons which in Nordic belief turns at the winter solstice or Yule. The upright line intersecting the circle signifies the two high points of the year at midwinter and midsummer.

It is a rune sacred to the Norns as rulers of time, and to the fertility god Frey, whose major festival was celebrated at the end of summer and coincided with the gathering in of the harvest. The pagan Old Religion was closely linked with agricultural cycle and the concept of the land as sacred. It would be wrong to regard these pagan beliefs as merely evidence of a primitive fertility cultus. Unlike the later dualistic religions, paganism recognized that spirit was immanent in matter. The natural progression of the seasons provided a metaphor for spiritual reality.

With the present environmental crisis, humankind is once more realizing that it is a part of Nature and not a separate creation. The dualistic teachings of Judaeo-Christianity, which have been accepted over the last 2,000 years and have coloured our perception of the natural world, can be seen as a doctrine which has attributed to the present negative view of our environment. In contrast, the pagan world view offers a vision of humanity living in harmony with Nature and respecting the Earth.

EOH

Death

The death rune was symbolized by the yew tree, which was also the best wood for carving runes. In Norse mythology the World Tree Yggdrasil was said to be a yew. For obvious reasons the yew is also a tree sacred to Odin in his role as sacrificed god.

In English folklore the yew tree has always been an omen of death and for this reason were planted in churchyards. They were said to protect the dead from graverobbers and prevent them haunting the living. In Christian belief the yew was a tree of resurrection for the dead would allegedly rise up from their graves on Judgement Day.

Today death is the final taboo and is seldom mentioned in polite company. In the often harsh reality of pagan society death was a frequent visitor to the hearthside. However once the idea is accepted that the physical body is only a temporary abode for the soul and that matter and spirit are indivisible, dying can no longer hold the same fear.

Death can be seen as a gateway opening to another state of existence. In northern European myths, the afterworld for warriors was visualized as the Great Hall of Valhalla where fires blazed all day and night, the tables were laden with food and the mead cups overflowed.

PEORTH

Hearth

This is an ambiguous rune which has been given several meanings. It has variously been translated as 'hearth', 'fruit tree' and 'chessmen'. It would appear to be connected with games of chance and therefore the

power of Wyrd. Alternatively, it can be
linked with sacred music, bardism and the
sacred dance.

In European pagan religion in general the bard played an
important role and was often also a shaman. He or she
was the person who could recollect the sacred songs and
the ceremonial dances passed down through the
generations which lay at the cultural heart of tribal belief.
In the Middle Ages the cloak of the pagan bard was worn
by the travelling minstrels and court jesters, who used folk
songs and bawdy jests to conceal the secrets of the old
ways.

EOLH

Protection

As its name suggests, this is a protection rune.
It derives its magical name from a species of
giant elk which used to roam the forests of
prehistoric Europe. It was used as a warning
device to keep trespassers off private property
and protect the wearer from harm. As its shape
dictates, it is also a feminine sign of the
Goddess.

The Eolh sigil would appear to be derived from a Germanic
hand gesture used to ward off evil spirits. If a person
believed they were being threatened by negative influences
they put out the palm of the hand facing outwards and
raised three fingers to psychically deflect the hostile energy.
This traditional sign of protection was probably connected
with the two fingered horned gesture used in the Middle
Ages to ward off the evil eye and as a recognition signal
between witches. Reversed and surrounded by a circle, it is
the logo of CND and symbolizes the enclosure and
neutralizing of negative phallic power represented by nuc-
lear weapons.

39

SIGIL

Sun

The title of this rune means quite literally 'the sun', which was an important object of worship in the Bronze and Iron Age cultures of northern Europe. Symbolically the sun represents the life force but in Germanic myth it was regarded as feminine. This gender reversal probably dates back to the matrifocal culture of pre-patriarchal times.

In prehistoric rock carvings the sun was often represented by the swastika or sun wheel. This is one of the most misunderstood of all ancient spiritual symbols. In the twentieth century its use by the National Socialists in Germany has tainted it with the aura of fascism. In fact the swastika is one of the oldest religious symbols known to humanity. It features in cave paintings dating from the Ice Age and can be found in the spiral designs of the Navajo and Hopi Indians in North America, the Celtic equal-armed cross and the flyfot national logo of the Isle of Man. In addition, the swastika is also found in Greece, Central and South America, China, Persia, Japan and India.

TYR

Tiw

Tyr, Tew or Tiw was one of the principal gods of the divine dynasty known as the Aesir, which included Odin and Thor. He was a deity of war and gave his name to our modern weekday Tuesday. From its shape the Tyr rune is obviously a phallic symbol. It denotes 'victory in battle' and represents martial values and attributes.

It would be wrong, however, to regard this rune as a symbol of destructive male energy. Tyr was a god who exemplified the forces of divine justice not the crude, macho philosophy of 'might is right'. In the final battle of

Ragnarok, which decides the destiny of the gods and the universe, Tyr binds the Fenris wolf who symbolizes the powers of chaos. In this fight the beast tears off the god of war's hand but is finally defeated and the cosmic order is preserved. The sacrifice made by Tyr indicates that he represents male energy channelled into a positive form.

BEORC

Birth

In rune lore Beorc signifies the birch tree, which is a symbol of fertility. Its shape resembles the female breasts. Beorc is also known as the 'birth rune' and is connected with fecundity, children and the Great Mother Goddess.

It is regarded as a lucky rune because often erotic symbols were used to dispel misfortune and attract good vibrations. Flagellation with birch twigs was once practised as a good luck charm and survives today in the traditional Scandinavian sauna. In some pagan rituals the altar was the naked body of the priestess of the Goddess who lay on a bed of birch twigs and wild flowers.

Birch trees were also believed to have healing powers and their leaves could be used in wort cunning to brew infusions which cured many complaints. In the shamanic tradition the red-capped toadstool *amanita muscaria* or fly agaric was employed to facilitate contact with the spirit world. It is often found growing underneath birches in the late summer or early autumn.

EH

Horse

The horse was sacred to the fertility god Frey and this divine animal is represented in the runic alphabet by Eh. Indo-European myth presents the horse as an important sacred beast and the Celtic and Saxon hill figures of southern England celebrate this fact.

In Norse religion Odin rode on an eight-legged steed called Sliepnir while, as we saw earlier in our discussion of the rune Rad, the sun was drawn across the sky in a wagon by two solar horses known as Earlwake and Allspirit. In pagan rituals the spirit horse carries the shaman to the Otherworld. Sacred horses were also kept by the Germanic priests for divination purposes. They made predictions by interpreting the noises the horses emitted.

MANNAZ

Man

Kinship and bloodlines were very important to the Aryan races of northern Europe. Each individual belonged to a clan to whom they owed primary loyalty and this extended beyond this life into the next world. Each tribe erected the mound where their kin would be buried and had to ensure they carried out the correct burial rites so the dead did not become 'nightwalkers' haunting the living.

These responsibilities of tribal life go back far before the Viking Age and originated in prehistoric ways of living. Often Indo-European royal houses traced their ancestry back to divine origins. As late as Anglo-Saxon England it was the custom for kings to claim descent from Odin.

Communal responsibility was a strong feature of family life in ancient times. While a degree of individuality was actively encouraged, it was also accepted that nobody could act in isolation. In a tribal unit the actions of a single person could not be viewed separately, for they ultimately affected everyone else. The only exception to this was the role of the tribal shaman who, as the intermediary between the community and the gods, was allowed to follow the path of the 'lone wolf'.

LAGU

Γ

Water

This is the water rune signifying a lake or the sea. The ocean is symbolically the womb of the Great Mother Goddess which is the source of all life in the universe. The association between the tides, the lunar cycle and menstruation is well known.

The Lagu rune is sacred to the sea god Njord and his consort the earth goddess Nerthus who was worshipped on an island sanctuary in the middle of a lake. The Vikings were a seafaring people and ship burials such as the famous one found at Sutton Hoo in Suffolk were common. Viking chiefs were also ritually cremated on longships which were set alight and allowed to drift out to sea as blazing tombs.

On an esoteric level this rune is said to awaken psychic powers and promote astral travel. For this reason it was sacred to the goddess Freyja who is traditionally credited with granting the wisdom of the runes to Odin. It is a fact that when women are menstruating they are at their most potent psychically and Lagu was used by the female seers whose patron was Freyja.

ING

◇

Fertility

This unusual rune is named after a mysterious god who was seen travelling over the water in a wagon by the East Danes. They at first thought he was the sea god Njord but he was later identified with Frey.

The rune is a symbol of fertility and its shape is said to represent the testicles. However, it could also be a bisexual symbol representing both the male and female genitalia. As such Ing symbolizes sexual polarity or the union of the opposites.

The Saxon kings of north-east Britain and the Swedish

43

royal family both claimed descent from the god Ing. It is believed the name England is derived from 'the land of Ing', and the word often prefixes Scandinavian names, for example the actress Ingrid Bergman.

DAEG

Dawn

The name of this rune refers to the dawn of a new day. This was an event welcomed in the northern lands especially after the long nights of winter. Where the sun was worshipped as a symbol of the life force its rising was ritually greeted each day.

Dawn and dusk are two of the most important magical times. At these periods the veil of the unseen between Middle Earth and the Otherworld is thinnest. The powers of light and darkness are at equal strength and it is a time for seeing the spirits of the dead, elves and the Old Gods.

Daeg is also the symbol of that time of the year when the power of the sun is at its strongest. This is the summer solstice or midsummer in mid-June when the sacred fires were lit on hilltops to worship the sun.

ODAL

Home

The Odal rune signifies the ancestral home. It is the special place from which the tribe or individual originated or their present homeland.The concept of the sacred landscape and the importance of the bloodline were key beliefs in the pagan world view.

In a modern society where it is almost a crime to be old we need the pagan idea that old people are sources of wisdom and traditional knowledge. The cult of the ancestral dead and the relationship between the king and the sacred land, personified by the earth goddess, were both integral aspects of pagan belief in ancient cultures worldwide.

This completes the magico-spiritual meanings of each rune and in the next chapter we will examine how the Norse and Germanic people used the runes, describe the major gods and goddesses of the Nordic pantheon and study the descriptions of the runes in the Norse sagas.

CHAPTER FOUR

USING RUNES

How did the ancient rune masters believe the runes worked? As there are no written records concerning runic magic (like most genuine occult knowledge the secrets of the runic alphabet were passed from person to person by word of mouth only) it is very difficult to find out why the Norse and Saxon people had such a strong belief in the potency of these strange mystical letters. They certainly regarded the runes as a special alphabet to be used only for magical purposes, healing, cursing and the wording of legal contracts or pacts between tribes or individuals which could never be broken.

We referred earlier to the elemental spirits associated with the runes which were regarded as the major source of their mysterious power. In some cases these entities are the gods and goddesses of the Old Norse religion. As runecraft faded under the baleful influence of the Christian Church and its black-robed priests, the once mighty gods of the north degenerated into lesser spirits, faeries or demons. There is an old saying,, which is very true, that the gods of the old religion become the devils of the new one, and the debasement of the pagan deities by Christianity is a prime example of this in action.

Nordic Gods

The gods of the Nordic pantheon were a larger than life, lusty crowd who seemed to have spent their time fighting, eating and drinking or indulging in orgiastic merry-making. They were therefore perfect reflections of the people who worshipped them. Originally, of course, the Stone Age people believed in the life force represented by a god and goddess known simply as the Lord and Lady. As religious concepts became more sophisticated the divine couple were sub-divided into a complete pantheon of gods and goddesses. Each deity symbolized a different aspect or attribute of the creative principles which had brought the universe into physical form. The principal deities who were worshipped by the northern Europeans are described below.

Thor

This deity is a typically Indo-European version of the thunder/sky god and is the eldest son of Odin. His magical weapon is a huge hammer or thunderbolt which is a symbol of phallic power. He uses it to protect the farms and houses of his devotees from the frost giants. Thor also possesses a magical belt with the power to double his strength and iron gloves enabling him to wield any weapon. His sacred totem animal is the goat.

Sif

Thor's wife is Sif, who is a deity associated with fertility and the harvest. Her long blonde hair is said to represent the fields of waving corn which can be seen in the late summer season.

Frigg

Frigga or Frigg is also a goddess of fertility and sexuality. For this reason she has lent her name as a slang word for female masturbation. As the consort of Odin she takes a prominent position in the Nordic pantheon. Her symbol is the distaff, which she uses to weave destinies like the Norns.

Freyja

Sometimes Freyja is confused with Frigg as she is the Norse goddess of love, but then love is often mixed up with sexual attraction. Freyja has many similarities with Odin as she follows the shamanic path, possesses psychic powers and has the magical ability to shapeshift. This goddess was the patron of the elite sisterhood of priest-esses known as the volvas, who were renowned for their prophetic utterances. These women seem to have been female shamans and were consulted on important tribal matters. The volvas had familiar spirits in the shape of cats (like the medieval witches) and the cat was Freyja's totem animal.

Frey

The god of fertility is the consort of Freyja, who was also his sister. He was sometimes known as Frodi or Fricco in ancient texts. Frey was the ruler of the elves, faeries and goblins in Norse folk myth and the deity who presided over the celebration of harvest.

Njord

The sea god Njord is the chief deity of the Vanir pantheon of deities whose worship was far older than the Viking period. Njord became the patron god and protector of the Nordic seafarers on their journeys to other lands. He is also the consort of the earth goddess Nerthus.

Nerthus

Nerthus is the earth mother of Norse mythology whose chthonic cult goes back to the Bronze Age and before. Figurines of a goddess identified with Nerthus or her priestesses have been discovered by archaeologists. She is represented by a long-haired woman displaying large earrings, her breasts are bare and she is wearing a short skirt.

Heimdall

This god is allegedly the son of nine maidens (possibly an ancient lunar goddess) and has unusual physical attributes including enhanced hearing and super eyesight. For this reason he took the position of the guardian of the Rainbow Bridge which links the heavenly realm of Asgard with Midgard. In his position as guardian, Heimdall acts as a messenger between the two worlds.

Idunn

This maiden/virgin goddess is the sister of Sif. Her task is to carry the sacred apples which the gods and goddesses must eat to retain their spiritual vitality. Without this special diet they will lose their immortality and become like ordinary mortals.

Skadi

A goddess of winter and death who may be associated with the goddess Hel who rules the underworld. Skadi was the first wife of the sea god Njord before he became the consort of Nerthus.

Loki

In Norse religion Loki is the nearest approximation to a principle of evil. He is a fire god who takes the role of cosmic joker, divine fool or trickster. Loki is the brother of Hel, Queen of the Dead.

Baldur

Baldur is the youngest and most beautiful of all the gods in the Norse pantheon. It is said his face shines like the sun, his hair is the colour of gold and his eyes glow with the blue of the summer sky. He was the son of Odin and Frigga, from whom he inherited wisdom and the love of Nature. His father engraved Baldur's tongue with speech runes so that he was the most eloquent talker among the gods.

The legend of Baldur justifies retelling in some detail as it provides some interesting keys to understanding pagan philosophy. His popularity and desire to be a peacemaker solving disputes among the gods and goddesses was deeply resented by Loki, who was also jealous of the young god's physical beauty. Loki began to plot Baldur's downfall, but his plans reached the ears of Frigg. She made all living things swear an oath that they would never harm her son. Only the mistletoe was overlooked by the goddess and did not make this promise. Frigg had ignored it because the plant clung to the oak and had no power of its own.

To prove that Baldur was immune from harm, Frigg told the other gods to hurl spears at Baldur and hit him with their swords. She was pleased to see he remained unharmed after these attacks, even when Thor struck him with his magical hammer. Loki, however, tricked Frigg into telling him that the mistletoe had not taken the oath. The fire god took a sprig of the plant and fashioned it into an arrow with the help of an elven smith. Loki took this to the blind god Hodur and told him to join the merry game played by the other gods and shoot the arrow at his brother Baldur.

Unwittingly duped by Loki, the blind god agreed and let fly the deadly mistletoe arrow. It struck Baldur in the heart and, ceasing to be immortal, he fell dying. Loki eventually confessed to the crime and was condemned to be chained to a rock for eternity while a snake spat venom in his face.

The Powers of Light and Darkness

Readers who have some previous knowledge of the pagan myths will recognize the elements in this story of the eternal conflict between the powers of darkness and the forces of light. In this case it is the young god of summer who is killed by the god of winter. The sun of course dies at midwinter when it sinks to its lowest point in the sky, around the shortest day or the winter solstice. Slowly the sun rises again and is reborn in its full glory at the highest solar point, marked by the longest day or the summer solstice. The ancient people celebrated these events with rituals of death and rebirth featuring priests who enacted the cosmological drama centred on the changing pattern of the seasons.

Baldur is the Norse version of the dying or sacrificed god whose death revitalizes Nature and fertilizes the earth. He can be either a solar deity or a god of vegetation. The story of this ritual murder can be duplicated in the myths of other pagan cultures. In Greece it is the young god Adonis who is killed by a wild boar and passes to the underworld. After the season of his death (winter) he is reborn and wild flowers bloom where his blood has been spilt. In Ancient Egypt it was Osiris who was murdered by his twin brother Set in a symbolic battle between good and evil. His partner and sister the goddess Isis gathers up the pieces of his dismembered body and Osiris is reborn as the lord of the underworld.

Sir James Frazer in his classic work of anthropology and folklore *The Golden Bough* (Macmillan & Co, 1890) has written extensively of this pagan motif. He tells of the sacred grove of the goddess Diana at Nemi which was guarded by a priest who used the title Rex Nemorensis or the King of the Woods. In the grove of the goddess was a mighty tree of which no branch might be broken, for it was taboo. Only a runaway slave was allowed to break off the sacred boughs of the tree. If he managed to do this he could challenge the guardian priest of the grove to single combat. If then he managed to kill the old priest then the slave automatically took his place as the hierophant of the mysteries of Diana.

Earlier we have seen the rites of human and animal sacrifice which surrounded the cult of Odin. This same theme dominates the life of his son Baldur and in many cases it seems as if the two gods are identical, merely old and young aspects of the one deity sharing a common bond of family and bloodletting. Certainly Dr William Chaney's theories concerning the descent of the Anglo-Saxon kings from Odin and their mysterious deaths resembling ritual killings (an idea also explored in great depth by the late Dr

Margaret Murray of University College, London) together with the ancient legend of divine priest kings such as Rex Nemorensis, suggest a very old religious or magical tradition coming down through the centuries from the dawn of pre-history.

The Norns

Although it was Odin who was said to have received the arcane wisdom of the runes hanging on the World Tree, the Norse folk often associated the magical alphabet with the powers of fate or destiny. This was called *Wryd* in Old Scandinavian and was the province of three goddesses known as the Norns. These goddesses were three sisters who weaved the fate of men on their looms. In Old English the words 'weave', 'destiny' and 'fortune' were often associated with each other in significant sentences which suggest some occult (i.e. hidden) meaning is implied by the writer or speaker.

After the conversion of the pagans to Christianity the Norns survived as folklore memories of the three Fates, as the ugly sisters in the pantomime *Cinderella* and in *Sleeping Beauty* as the wicked witch with the poisoned spinning wheel. Perhaps the most melodramatic representation of these old Nordic goddesses is the three witches on the blasted heath in Shakespeare's play *Macbeth*. He describes them as 'weird sisters' who could foretell the truth in the tradition of the pagan Norse seeresses.

In the mythology of the northern folk the Norns were known by their personal names of Urd, Verdanki and Skuld. They personified the past, the present and the future respectively. They were therefore invoked by the rune masters before they divined the future by casting the runic letters. The Norns also guarded the Yggdrasil or World Tree which supports the earth. Every morning they poured a libation of mead over its roots so that its leaves would stay green. From this libation comes the honey dew which drips on the earth and is stored by the bees. The Norns had in their service fair maidens who materialized in dreams to impart advice and guidance. These maids also had the task of finding willing mothers for unborn babies to incarnate in.

It would seem that the personification of the Norns resembled in many ways the triple aspect of the Great Goddess which is found in nearly every pagan religion; the maiden, the mother and the old crone. Urd was said to be very old and looked backward over her shoulder, as old people often do. Verdanki was a young girl and gazed straight ahead into the present. Lastly, Skuld was said to be veiled and had an unopened scroll on her lap which contained the secrets of the future. Her description sounds very much like that of The High Priestess card in the gypsy Tarot pack which is sometimes used for fortune-telling. In the occult teachings of the Tarot — which have nothing to do with their usage as a way of predicting coming events — the card of The High Priestess or Papess symbolizes inspiration, memory and divine prophecy. She is the medium through which the gods or archetypal forces speak to the material world.

Magical Uses of the Runes

Although today we principally regard the runes as a method of divination, in the past they possessed a multiplicity of magical uses. There were birth runes, health runes, death runes, battle runes, fertility runes, weather runes, love runes and cursing runes. Much of the old runic knowledge has been lost to us today but from archaeological sources we can rediscover the uses of the runes in magic and daily life.

Runes were frequently used to ward off grave robbers from the burial mounds of important tribal personages such as chiefs and high priests. It was stipulated that these protection runes had to be carved 'not by day and not by iron'. This seems a rather odd superstition but, like most, it is embedded in magical common sense (even if that seems a contradiction in terms to some people). The hours of darkness were the obvious time to practise necromantic rites and iron was the only metal which could frighten away departed spirits or the faery folk. Therefore its use was forbidden in or around burial places.

This belief dates back to the early days when the people who used iron conquered the tribes who still boasted bronze weapons and tools. The Bronze Age folk — a small, dark-skinned and hairy people — were regarded by the invaders as faeries and the superstitious said that they were scared of the magic metal iron. (Possibly for a good, practical reason, for iron can slice through the soft metal of a bronze sword blade.) Hence the tradition grew up that faeries or demons could be destroyed by iron, which they mortally feared to touch.

Runes of War

Staying with weapons of war we find that runes were often engraved on swords. An iron sword excavated on the Isle of Wight had inscribed on its blade in runic letters the legend: 'Woe to the weapons of the foe.' It also had carved in runes its rather bloodchilling name 'Increase to Pain', which is a pretty accurate description of its use in battle to deal death and injury to the enemy. Another example of sword runes are to be found on a broken blade dredged up from the River Thames. It is over two feet in length and engraved along it are the 28 letters of a runic alphabet and the name of its owner.

An ancient scabbard unearthed at Tonsberg bears the runic inscription 'Servant of the god'. It does not name him but we can feel sure that the deity referred to is the god of war, Tiw. On a buckle found near the sword was carved the motto 'I dedicate to the god' which suggests that the weapon was either a sacrificial sword or belonged to a *berserker* who dedicated the souls of his victims to Odin. On a short sword from Kragehul the warrior's name has been carved in runes together with the debatable words, 'I bring luck.' It certainly would not bring luck to those who died by its blows.

Runes of Escape

Another use for runes was to escape from your enemies if you were captured after a battle. The Christian historian Bede, writing in 679 CE, tells of a young Northumbrian captive who slipped his fetters and escaped. When he was recaptured he was asked in Old English, 'Hwae-oer he pa alysendlecam rune cuoe an pa stafs mid him awritene haefde?' Translated this means, 'Do ye know of the loosening runes and do you have the [magical] letters written about you?' Evidence that this was a popular form of runic magic is given by the words of the old god Odin himself who says, 'This fourth [runic] skill I know. If men put fetters on my limbs I chant such a charm that will let me escape from them.'

In an Old English charm the user of runes is also told by the hooded god, 'If you wish to go to your king or any other man then bear these runic staves. Each will be gracious and kind to you.'

Runes in Norse Sagas

Runes it seems had unlimited magical powers as the following extracts from the Norse saga illustrate:

Runes of war now thee,
if great thou wilt be,
cut them on hilt of hardened sword,
some on the brand's back,
some on its shining side,
twice the name Tiw therein.

Sea runes good at need,
learnt for ship's saving,
for the good health of the swimming horse;
on the stern cut them,
cut them on the rudder blade,
and set flame the shaven oar,
how so big the sea hills,
how so big the blue beneath,
hail from the main and then
comest thou home.

Word runes learn ye well
if thou wilt that no man,
pay back grief for the grief gavest,
wind thou these, cast thou these
all about you,
At the Thing where folk throng,
until the doom faring.

Of ale runes know the wisdom
if thou wilt another man's wife
should not betray thine heart that trusteth;
cut them on mead horn,
on the back of each hand
and nicked upon the nail.

Help runes shalt thou gather
if skill thou woulds't gain
to loosen chold from low-lain mother;
cut they be in hands hollow,
wrapped the joints round about,
call for the good folks gainsome help.

Learn the bough rune's wisdom
if leechlore thou lovest
and wilt wot about wounds searching,
on the bank they be scored,
on the buds of trees
whose boughs look eastward ever.

Thought runes shalt thou deal with,
if thou wilt be of all men,
fairest souled, right and wise
those creded, those first cut,
those took first to heart.

On the shield were they scored
that stands before the Shining God,
on Early-Waking's oar,
on All Knowing's hoof,
on the wheel which runneth under
Regnir's chariot,
on Sleipnir's jaw teeth,
on the sleigh traces,

on the rough bear's paw,
on Bragi's tongue,
on the wolf's claw,
on the eagle's bill,
on bloody wings,
and bridge's end,
on loosing palms
and pity's path.

On glass, on gold
and goodly silver,
in wine and wort
and the seat of the witch wife,
on Gungir's point
and Grani's bosom,
on the Norn's snail
and the neb of the night owl.

All these so cut
were shaven and sheared
and mingled with hold mead
and sent upon wide ways enow,
some abide with the elves,
some abide with the Aesir
or with the wise Vanir
or some still hold the
sons of mankind.

These be the book runes
and the runes of good help,
and all the ale runes
and the runes of much might
To whom so they may avail
unbewildered, unspoilt.
They are wholesome to hear,

thine thou with these then,
when thou has heard their lore,
till the Gods end thy life days.
                    Volsunga Sage

This poem illustrates the many and varied magical uses of runes, most of which have been unfortunately lost to us today and are only just being rediscovered. Further information on the many uses of the magical runes is given in the following epic poem which is said to have been composed by Odin for the guidance of his disciples the rune masters:

Know how to cut them,
know how to read them,
know how to stain them,
know how to evoke them,
know how to send them —
the Runes!

Better not to ask them to overpledge,
as a gift demands a gift,
better not to slay,
than to slay too many.

The first charm I know
is unknown to all of any human kind,
'Help' it is named
for help it gives
in hours of anguish
and in sorrow.

I know a second —
that those who would
be leeches must learn.

I know a third —
in battle if need be great,
it blunts the swords of
enemies so there are
no wounds.

I know a fourth —
which frees me quickly
if foes should bind me first,
and chant know I
that breaks fetters,
burst bonds.

A fifth — know I,
no crow hunts,
no spear kills,
no stone hurts.

I know a sixth —
if runes are cut
to harm me,
the spell is turned —
the hunter harmed not I.

I know a seventh rune,
if a hall blazes around
my bench mates,
though hot the flames
they feel nought.

I know an eighth —
if hate festers in
a warrior's heart,
my spell will calm him.

I know a ninth —
when need of it,
to shelter my ship in winter's storm,
the wind it calms,
the sea it puts to sleep.

I know a tenth rune —
if spirits trouble I work;
they wander afar,
unable to find form or home.

I know an eleventh —
when I lead in battle
and unwounded go to war,
unscathed I return.

I know a twelfth —
when I see aloft a tree
a corpse swing from a rope,
then I cut and paint runes
so the man walks,
speaks with me.

I know a thirteenth —
if I cast runes,
no warrior dies in battle
or falls by the sword.

I know a fourteenth —
that few know,
if I tell a troop of
warriors about the Old Ones,
gods and elves
I can name them all.

I know a fifteenth —
sung to the Gods it
gives power to men,
prowess to elves,
foresight to all by
Odin's gift.

I know a sixteenth —
that binds the hearts
and charms the young girls
releasing love.

I know a seventeenth rune —
that is never told,
a secret hidden from all,
except my love in my arms
and my sister.

Misuse of the Runes

This impressive list of magical powers has a hidden sting in its tail. One line says 'Better not to ask them to overpledge, as a gift demands a gift'.

At first glance perhaps innocent words — or are they really? It is in fact a subtle warning not to misuse the magic of the runes. Ask only for what you need because if you are greedy the powers-that-be will exact from you a tribute which you may not willingly pay. It is an old belief, based on cold fact, that if you are too successful in life or too lucky then something you love will be taken from you by the gods as the price for your success.

Such a belief is at the heart of the medieval tales concerning magicians who allegedly made pacts with the Devil in exchange for material wealth and happiness. At the conclusion of the bargain the magus, no matter how skilled he might be in theurgy, always loses and is forced reluctantly to mortgage his soul to the powers of darkness. As intelligent and educated people we no longer believe in the Christian bogeyman who at the witching hour rides up on a scarlet horse to claim our mortal spirit. However, such a belief in the untrustworthy gods and the sacrifices required of those who dabbled with the hidden forces of Nature is essentially pagan and predates the fairy tales of Christianity by many thousands of years. It is the ancient law encapsulated in the superstitious words of the wise who seeing someone inherit money say, 'No good will come of it.' The tragic circumstances which often surround winners of large sums on the football pools prove the truth of this old adage.

Also in the verses above is the chilling phrase 'better not to slay, than to slay too many'. This refers to the negative aspect of the runes as an instrument of magical murder. However, anyone foolish enough to use the runes for this purpose will soon encounter that other ancient law of magic that curses rebound three times over on the sender. This may not happen immediately but eventually the person who misuses the runes — or indeed any form of practical occultism — will have to face the severe consequences of his or her impulsive act. Nature has a way of dealing with those mere mortals who set themselves up as judge and jury over their fellow human beings and it is not a very pleasant fate to suffer.

On a lighter note, it is worth noting that not all runic inscriptions were of a magical significance. Sad to relate there were a few brave individuals who used them for less exalted purposes. When Viking raiders, under the leadership of Rognvaldr Kali, invaded the Orkneys in 1151 CE they left behind runic graffiti in the prehistoric burial

mound of Maes Howe. It records that a great treasure was
carried off from the place by the invading troops. In 1153
the Viking wanderers returned to the island and carved
more runes telling of a snow storm which stopped them
sailing and how two of their number went insane.

CHAPTER FIVE

RUNIC SURVIVALS

The heyday of the rune magicians was in the so-called Dark Ages after the Romans left Britain and it was invaded by Vikings, Danes and Saxon war bands. Our modern vision of the Vikings is one of uncouth barbarians who raped and looted their way across England during one of the darkest periods of the island's history. The truth, as is often the case with modern accounts of pagan peoples, is somewhat different. It had been revealed recently through historical research and archaeological excavations that the Vikings were a cultivated and civilized race who do not deserve the bloodthirsty image which popular films and sensational novels have given them. Their jewellery is second to none in fine craftsmanship and artistry and recent excavations at York have revealed that the Vikings were the merchants of the ancient world. Rows of shops have been unearthed where merchants from all over the Continent travelled to exchange wares and trade in wool, precious metals and weapons. The Nordic people occupied large areas of England and left their trademark today in the survival of local folk customs, place-names and even the racial characteristics of the inhabitants. They administered these tracts of land right up to the Norman conquest, which was basically the result of a family squabble between rival pagan tribes fighting for the English crown.

Anglo-Saxon and Norse England is generally regarded by historians as a debased, barbaric country. However the Saxons were capable of exquisite works of art. These include the famous Kingston brooch found in Kent. Dating from the seventh century CE it consists of a concentric design relieved by a cruciform pattern decorated with roundels and bosses. It uses gold, garnet, blue glass and white sea shell for relief. This brooch is a true example of Saxon workmanship at its best and proves the lie to the claims of those who dismiss the Saxon and Norse periods of English history as 'the Dark Ages'.

Absorption of Paganism

In our study of the magical runes we should also remember that the transition period from the practice of the pagan Old Religion and the conversion to Christianity was far longer than orthodox historians and theologians would have us believe. It was certainly not a case of waving a magic wand and everyone became Christian overnight as many history books suggest. While the aristocracy may have been convinced of the political power offered by the new religion, the country folk — who were the real pagans — refused to accept the teachings from the East and clung tenaciously to their old beliefs.

Realizing this, the Christian priests adapted the old ways to their religious beliefs and effectively negated them by absorption. Pope Gregory wrote to one of his British missionaries in the following words outlining how the Old Religion could be destroyed from within by his disciples:

> The idols amongst the people should on no account be destroyed but the temples themselves should be aspersed with holy water, altars to Christ set up in them and relics deposited therein. For if these heathen temples are well built they should be purified from the worship of demons and dedicated to the greater service of God. In this way the people, seeing their temples are not destroyed, may abandon their error and flock more readily to their accustomed resorts and there may come to know and adore the true God.

Such propaganda even influenced the followers of pagan rune magic. Some were quite happy to accept Jesus as another aspect of Odin. After all, the new god also hung on a tree and ritually died for the sins of his tribe. This was an eternal motif understood by all pagan peoples who knew of the sacrifice of the divine king who died to fertilize the earth with his blood. They therefore had no hesitation in accepting the mother of the Jewish divine king, Mary, as another aspect of the Great Goddess.

Dual Faith

During the period of Dual Faith which existed up to the eleventh and twelfth century CE runes became a mystical alphabet used to describe the life of Jesus and his disciples. A classic example is the Ruthwell Cross in a churchyard at Dumfries. This is inscribed with runes telling the story of the crucifixion intermingled with pagan symbols such as birds, animals and wild flowers. It also includes scenes from the nativity, the flight by Mary and Joseph to Egypt, the baptism of John, the healing of a blind man by the Nazarene and Mary Magdalene washing his feet.

On a coffin made for St Cuthbert in 698 CE runes and Roman letters are used side by side. Runes are especially used for the names of Jesus and the four apostles, Matthew, Mark, Luke and John. This is a survival of the pre-Christian practice of using the runes for the sacred names of the gods. That they were still in use for the tomb inscription of a seventh-century Christian holy man proves that their magical power had not diminished with the coming of the new religion.

Christian prayers often used pagan incantations, merely changing the names of the old pagan gods to those of saints and apostles. The folklorist Alexander Carmichael (1832-1912) spent a lifetime collecting Gaelic prayers and blessings still in common usage in the Scottish Highlands and the Hebrides. Many of these are thinly disguised pagan incantations for good harvests or the consecration of the seed. As well as calling on Jesus and the saints the prayers also invoke St Bride, who is a Christianized version of the Celtic goddess of sacred fires and holy wells, Bridget. Examples of these prayers can be found in Carmichael's book *The Sun Dances* (Floris Books, Edinburgh).

In one famous case of this type the Lord's Prayer, written in runes, was used by pagan Saxons as a battle charm. As late as the eleventh century (when historians would have us believe that Christianity was the omnipotent religion of Western Europe and paganism was a forgotten superstition) an Abbot Aelfric was forced to condemn 'outh drycraft oe runstafum' or the use of magic by means of the runes.

Earlier, during the eighth and ninth centuries CE, some rural graveyards boasted headstones carved with runic prayers to the dead. One of the most amazing examples of the fusion of paganism with Christianity is the famous

Franks casket which dates from this period of Dual Faith. It is named after Sir Augustus Franks who presented it to the British Museum in 1867. The casket features representations of Saxon pagan religion alongside scenes from the Bible, both described in the magical alphabet of the runes.

The front of the casket has on its left side an illustration depicting the Saxon god Wayland in his smithy — popularly supposed to be a neolithic burial mound near Uffington earthworks in Berkshire — complete with anvil, hammer and bellows. He holds in his metalworking tongs a human head which is to be made into a skull drinking cup. The headless body of its owner lies beneath the god's anvil. Two female assistants stand nearby and outside a young boy (possibly Wayland's brother Egil) is shown catching geese.

On the right of the casket can be seen the three magi or astrologers kneeling with gifts before the Virgin Mary and her new-born baby. Above shines the star over Bethlehem. Each of the pictures is surrounded by a border of runic characters which explains each one.

Healing Charms

It is probable that the secrets of the runes were kept alive by the Anglo-Saxon physicians who practised leechcraft. This involved the use of magical charms, healing herbs and incantations which combined pagan and Christian prayers. An example of a pagan-Christian healing charm is given below:

Our Lord Woden rade,
his foal's foot slade

down he lighted
his foal's foot righted,
bone to bone, flesh to flesh,
heal in the name of
Woden, Baldur and Freyja.
Baldur and Woden
fared to the wood,
there was to Baldur's foal
his foot wrenched,
then charmed Woden
as well he knew how,
as for bone wrench,
so for limb wrench,
bone to bone,
limb to limb
as if they were glued.

Another example of a Norse Saxon charm derived from runic magic is the following which was used to cure burns. It mentions the Norns and the major gods of the Nordic pantheon:

Three ladies came out of the east,
with snow, frost and fire,
out fire — in frost,
in the names of Woden, Thor and Loki.

This fusion of pagan and Christian belief illustrates the struggle in Anglo-Saxon England between the rival faiths. It was the battle of minds, souls and hearts which reached up from peasant cottage to the halls of the kings who claimed descent from Woden. It ended in bloody strife, for as soon as the Church gained political power it suppressed the heretics in its ranks and the unbelievers outside its kingdom who chose to follow different spiritual paths.

Persecution of Pagans

In the late fourteenth century the first major witchcraft trials began and during the next 400 years it is estimated that several million men, women and children died to satisfy the Church's insane revenge against the pagans. Many innocents were among those who went to their deaths on the pyre or gibbet. Faced with such horrific tortures as the eye gougers, thumb screws and the rack many chose a false confession and a quick death to the prolonged agony of the Inquisition.

Condemnation of the runes as symbols of black magic was a result of the medieval witch hunts. By the end of the Middle Ages rune lore was largely forgotten. The word *rune* had degenerated to mean any magical word or symbol used in a spell or incantation. It was not until the late nineteenth century that runes once more appeared in public consciousness and this was the result of research by German occultists who were trying to revive Teutonic and Norse paganism.

Political Paganism

Many of these occultists identified themselves with various extreme forms of German nationalism. One of these was Dr Benhard Koerner, a member of the Prussian Herald's Office and an expert on the genealogy of old German families. Koerner became a member of the Germanen Order in 1912. This was an extreme right wing group combining anti-Semitic politics with occultism and rune magic. It had revived the Mysteries of Odin and its initiates were introduced to the fraternity by a ritual resembling those practised in the pagan temples of pre-Christian Europe. The initiate was told he was a member of a superior race and told to kiss the blade of a sword as a symbolic gesture of allegiance to the Order. One of the first spiritual teachings he was given was the meaning of the magical runic alphabet.

Koerner was a disciple of the famous German occultist and rune master Guido von List (1848-1919) whose book *The Secrets of the Runes* was a bestseller in European occult circles. List had experienced a childhood vision in St Stephen's cathedral in Vienna during which he travelled back in time to a historical period when he alleged it had been a temple to Woden. From that moment the young List dedicated his life to promoting northern European paganism.

In his twenties List worked as a journalist writing about myths, fairy tales and folklore. He also cultivated extreme right wing political views based on German nationalism and became a member of the Theosophical Society. In the 1890s List revived the cult of Woden, organized rituals to celebrate the solstices and wrote plays with mythological themes. In 1903 List discovered the runes in mysterious circumstances after suffering temporary blindness following an eye operation.

List also began to study heraldry and genealogy shortly after this event. He became convinced the ancient families of Europe were descendants of the old priesthood of Woden. Following his study of medieval secret societies, List also came to believe that occult fraternities such as the Knights Templar, the Freemasons and the Rosicrucians had inherited the secrets of runecraft from pagan times.

In 1908 he created the List Society to promote his theories to a wider audience. This organization had a membership which included intellectuals, writers, artists, poets, occultists, Spiritualists, Theosophists, army officers and nationalist politicians who shared List's interest in the runic alphabet. Although membership of the society was open to the public, List also formed an inner circle composed of trusted disciples called the Armanen Order. This esoteric group practised rune magic and neo-pagan rituals to celebrate the seasonal cycle.

Today the teachings of Guido von List have influenced the revival of interest in the runes which began in the late 1970s. His book *The Secret of the Runes* has recently been reprinted (Destiny Books, US, 1989). With this revived interest in the runes has come a resurgence of the worship of the old Norse gods and goddesses. Since the 1950s various forms of neo-paganism have been re-established in Western Europe, the United States and Australia. This revival movement includes small groups of people who are practising the northern European pagan tradition.

Among the most prominent of these Nordic neo-pagans are the Odinic Rite and the English Odinist Hof in Britain and the Fellowship of Asatru in the United States. In Iceland the Norse version of neo-paganism has been officially recognized as a legitimate religion by the government. This is due to intense campaigning by local Odinists who call themselves the *Asatruarmean* or the Believers in the Aesir.

These modern groups of Nordic neo-pagans have been joined by practitioners of Wicca who follow a Saxon form of paganism. In 1974 an American Wiccan, who had been initiated by the late Gerald Gardner, published a complete set of rituals for what he called the Seax Wica tradition. This was based on Gardnerian Wicca but incorporated runelore and the worship of Woden and Freyja. In Norway another group of witches are also said to worship these deities but they claim that this is not a revived cult but the survival of pre-Christian pagan practices which have continued into the modern age.

CHAPTER SIX

THE MAGIC OF RUNES

Magic is probably the most misunderstood word in the human language. If you do not believe that statement ask your friends and work mates what the word means to them. Their answers will be revealing and show just how low the true magical arts have degenerated since their pagan heyday.

Today, magic is associated in the minds of the general public with party conjurers producing rabbits out of top hats, wicked witches waving toytown wands in pantomimes or obscene rites in lonely country churchyards. Each of these images is a modern cliché and none of them is in any way representative of true magic or the people who practise it. In the past one did not have to explain what magic was to the majority of people. They encountered it and its effects in everyday life. It was accepted without question that there were certain people who were apart from the common herd, different in a way which could only be understood if you accepted that the material world and the realms of spirit were aspects of one unity. These people possessed strange powers and had unusual knowledge; they could see into the future, read minds and even manipulate the elemental forces of nature. Their powers could be used for evil but in the majority of cases they were respected members of the community who could be called upon to help those in need.

Today we have invented a brand new technical terminology to describe these powers which our ancestors took for granted. We call them extra-sensory perception, parapsychology, precognition, out-of-the-body experiences and telekinesis. Even our feeble attempts to rationalize these powers by giving them pseudo-scientific names cannot disguise how little we really know about them. Nowadays a scientifically-educated psychic researcher or 'parapsychologist' would laugh at you if you insisted on describing his field of study as 'magic' or 'magical' but it was so regarded by our forebears and who is to say they were wrong to do so?

Denial of the Pagan View

In earlier chapters the shamanistic tradition has been described. It is a magico-religious belief system which, at first glance, seems to belong to a backward phase of human history when dark superstition and cruel barbarism ruled the lives of humanity. In fact this concept of our pagan past is one that has been forced upon us by conditioning. An insidious and sinister form of conditioning which is inherent in our educational system, which colours the view of the outside world presented to us each morning by the newspapers and on the evening television news. A conditioning process which permeates the scientific and technological establishment and distorts the real truth about the relationship between humans and their physical environment.

Those spiritual anarchists, the shamans, were not conditioned by any man-made force seeking to manipulate their vision of the outside reality. Unlike ourselves they had not been subjected to the theories of Sir Isaac Newton or the philosophy of Descartes who conceived the universe according to a mechanical model which had been constructed by an omnipotent, supreme creator in the manner of a Swiss watch. Since Newton it has been the traditional scientific stance to separate matter from spirit and this reached the height of its absurdity in the Victorian era of rationalism when spirit was finally denied and rejected.

The scientific establishment rejected the pagan view that the Earth is a living organism, that all life in the universe is permeated by the creative energy of the life force and that everything that exists is part of a greater oneness. The pagans knew and accepted this fundamental fact just as they knew and accepted magic. Their belief in the essential oneness of life and the shamans' concept of the Earth as a living entity are graphically illustrated by the following quotation extracted from the works of a medieval pagan philosopher Basilius Valentinus:

> The Earth is not a dead body but is inhabited by the
> spirit that is its life and soul. All created things draw
> their strength from the Earth spirit. This spirit is life, it
> is nourished by the stars and it gives nourishment to
> all living things it shelters in its womb.

These are words which would have been easily recognized by the oldtime shaman or rune master. Even today they would be acceptable to the surviving magicians of the various ethnic races who still cling tenaciously to the Old Ways despite the spiritual coercion of the missionaries and the material inducements of multi-national companies who have made it their goal to enlighten our brethren of the Third World.

Rejection of Rationalism

Today, when so many people have found the technological dream crumbling around us in crime, vandalism and the pollution of the Earth, the old shamanistic ideas are once more beckoning us in the West. The Newtonian-Cartesian-Darwinian theories are being ruthlessly examined and found to be wanting. As the American writer and philosopher Gary Snyder has said recently, it is time at this crucial period in human history to return to the roots of our religious origins. Awareness of what we are doing to our environment by increased industrialism is forcing a new look to be given to the accepted values which arose with the Cartesian philosophy. Snyder has pointed out that a book such as *Black Elk Speaks* (Abacus Books, 1974), written by a North American shaman, is recognized by many people today as the testament of a spiritual philosophy which predates Judaeo-Christianity and the Hindu-Buddhist religion by many thousands of years. It is a philosophy which teaches that humanity cannot separate itself from its physical environment or the matters of the spirit. Each is a reflection of the great oneness which the ancient shamans recognized and tuned into in order to gain their magical powers.

These magical powers belong to a world which has been largely ignored during the last 200 years of material rationalism. Today a few pioneering scientists, such as Dr Fritjof Capra, who has taught us a new system of metaphysical science based on mystical physics, are opening our eyes to a new non-mechanical theory of the universe. We are rediscovering the old shamanistic view of the cosmos and realizing that all life is an eternal, flowing movement of change and transformation, a cosmic dance of the heavens. The universe can be perceived as the final manifestation of an ultimate reality pattern. It is sustained by a unifying essence with a central function to manifest in myriad forms, which come into being, evolve, disintegrate and are then rebuilt in an everlasting cycle of existence.

The Central Truths

At various stages in human history this central truth has either been lost or misunderstood. Our present materialistic age is one of these dark periods. In the past the priesthood, who were the guardians of magical knowledge, knew that the mass of people had largely lost the ability to conceive of the oneness of all life (although a few initiates like the shamans still retained the knowledge). Because of this, three levels of religious expression were developed and humanity began to visualize the godhead on three levels of understanding.

These were: *the Supreme Creative Principle* — pure, asexual, transcendental energy, sometimes simply referred to as the life force; *the Creative Duality* — the life force manifesting symbolically as a god and goddess representing the masculine and feminine aspects of the human psyche, and *the Archetypes* — magical images of the god and goddess as mythological deities, racial heroes and cultural teachers. The Nordic, Celtic, Roman, Greek, Egyptian and Hindu religions are based on the latter concept and feature gods who, at some early period of the culture's history, were real people living on earth. The Archetypes, according to the Swiss psychologist Dr Carl Jung, represent fundamental human qualities and desires which appear in dreams, myths, visions and folklore.

It should be understood that these Archetypes are subjective personifications of the Supreme Creative Principle of Life Force. However, some occult philosophers claim that they can possess a separate reality outside the realms of human imagination. They claim that the gods are visualized by their human worshippers with such intense concentration that they can become a focus for natural forces seeking manifestation on the material plane. The famous occultist Dion Fortune said that a god is an artificial thought-form built up over long periods of time by successive generations. When the magician or shaman visualizes the image of the god in his or her mind it is the corresponding aspect of his or her nature which gives it power and form.

That the various gods and goddesses invoked in ritual magic (and that includes, for the purpose of this book, the magic of the runes) possess a separate existence as artificial thought forms or elementals is an idea explored by the writer Hzhak Bentov. He even describes the *modus operandi* of creating a god. Bentov imagines a rock in a desert. This inanimate (yet not 'dead' as we understand the term) object has a low level of consciousness. Its threshold of conscious awareness is stimulated by contact with small animals in the vicinity who regard the rock as a protector against the elements and bigger animals. When a human being travels through the desert who is sensitive to Nature he or she finds that there is something 'different' about the stone. If this person is of a culture which follows the animistic old religion, or is sympathetic to such influences, his or her awe of the rock may turn into direct worship of it as a cult object and the habitat of a friendly (or in some cases unfriendly) spirit. This attention boosts the rock's embryonic consciousness even further and eventually the spirit of the stone is transformed into a god.

Manifestations of the Life Force

The belief in spirits which reside in stones is worldwide and can best be experienced in the practices of the Toraja tribe who are scattered across the islands of the Indonesian archipelago. They have set up huge megalithic monuments which today are 'fed' with pig blood but in the past were honoured by human sacrifices. Some of the strange reports of 'supernatural' happenings in the vicinity of European stone circles may be explained by Bentov's theories. Certainly the old idea that stone is an inactive, solid mass has been revised by the latest discoveries in physics which suggest that it is a complex energy structure with many amazing secrets to offer us.

What Bentov is describing in his story of the rock in the desert is the creation of an elemental, faery or Nature spirit which is associated with the manifestation of the life force through organic matter. These energy forces have been worshippéd in the past as minor gods or the spirit guardians of sacred wells, trees, standing stones, lakes and rivers. Such forces have the ability to tune in to the human mind and cause it to interpret them in archetypal images. An example of this process was given to the author by the late W. E. Butler. Visiting an ancient site he saw a small sphere of light hovering over one of the stones. From his experience as a practising occultist he recognized this phenomena as the manifestation of a Nature spirit. His companion, who was not clairvoyantly trained and lacked any magical knowledge, also saw the spirit. However, she described it as taking the traditional shape of a faery as depicted in children's story books. This experience suggests that in some unknown way we are conditioned to receive aspects of the spiritual reality in specifically constructed archetypal forms. It may also offer an explanation for the modern UFO phenomenon which may have very little to do with close encounters with little green men from Mars but a lot to do with the faery kingdoms and the so-called 'dragon power' which occultists and dowsers say is channelled across the countryside between prehistoric sites along the mysterious ley lines.

The Multi-Visioned View

The theory of the universe described above coincides with the recent research work completed by two leading physicists, Karl Pribham of the Stanford University in the United States and David Bohm of London University. They allege that our brains mathematically construct what we call reality by interpreting frequencies from a level of primal existence which transcends time and space. This archetypal reality pattern they liken to a universal hologram (i.e. a type of photograph that produces a three-dimensional image). They further suggest that phenomena such as magic, precognition, telepathy, time warps, ESP and mystical experience are an aspect of the primal reality and occur when certain people tune in, either accidentally or consciously, to the Universal Matrix which sustains the cosmic hologram.

We seem to have come a long way from the meaning of magic; but not really, for the shaman or rune magician are both examples of people with the above average ability to tune in, either accidentally or consciously, to the Universal Matrix or spirit world and reactivate those powers of the mind which lie dormant in most other members of the human race. The shaman or rune magician is a multi-visioned entity in contrast to the average person in Western technological society who suffers from that blindness of the spirit which the poet William Blake described as 'single vision'.

Writing in the popular American science magazine *Omni* in the late 1970s, Kenneth Brower speculated on exactly why humanity seems to have lost its collective footing on the path to progress by means of technological supremacy over the forces of Nature. He thinks that the Judaeo-Christian edict in the Bible instructing human beings to increase and multiply in order to subdue Nature and the animal kingdom is one of the root causes of our modern predicament. Brower believes, like the old shamans, that our attitude to the earth was far healthier when we were pagans and believed spirits resided in everything, when humans and animals were on equal terms and trees had to be placated before cutting. In fact, Brower is advocating the multi-visioned view of the natural world as opposed to the single vision.

The Sixth Sense

It is a well-known fact that we use only a small percentage of our total available brain power. A great deal of its potency lies submerged in the shadows of the unconscious mind. In prehistoric times it is certain that humanity was far more developed on the intuitive level than we are today. The sensory organs of sight, smell, touch, taste and hearing were far more sharpened, as befits primitive men who hunted for their living and faced daily danger from wild animals and other humans who would have cheerfully killed them without compassion.

Gradually, as humanity became more civilized, and moved into an era of towns, villages and cities, the so-called sixth sense — the intuitive part of the brain — ceased to function and slowly its powers degenerated. They survived in flashes of inspiration, psychic visions in times of stress or prophetic dreams. This process occurred over a long period of time but has accelerated in our own society during the last 200 years due to our rapid industrialization and retrograde retreat from natural life styles. But some members of the human race (not only in the ethnic areas of the world isolated from the malefic influences of the industrial society) have managed to preserve the magical multi-vision despite pressures from the single-visioned technocrats to conform to the status quo.

Social Conditioning

Young children are naturally psychic and will often talk of invisible playmates. Such talk is usually dismissed by unenlightened parents as the product of infantile imaginations. In fact, children who repeatedly tell tales about faeries or angels may be treated as pathological liars or mentally deficient. Faced with such a prospect children soon learn to stay silent for to speak openly of such natural happenings is to invite the ridicule and contempt of grown-ups. This process is reinforced when the child reaches school age for there is no place in our modern education system for the dreamer, poet or visionary. Education today (except in some progressive schools where the pupils are allowed, indeed encouraged, to develop their artistic and creative talents) is geared to producing nicely-conditioned zombies who will become the technologists and factory fodder of our brave new industrial world.

In the past no such inhibitions were placed on the person who claimed to have visions or had the power to make things happen. They were regarded as important people whose natural awareness of the spirit world was a valuable contribution to the community. When Christianity became the dominant religion of Western Europe (and, as previously mentioned, it did not do so without a long struggle with paganism which lasted hundreds of years), the psychic and the magician became the outcasts of society.

Invoking the Power of the Runes

Returning to the special magical powers of the runic alphabet — how can the average person today, who wishes to escape from the limits of single vision existence, tap the occult power of the runes?

Rune magic, like all practical occult techniques, can be dangerous. Great caution is required and the runes should *never* be treated as an amusing parlour game, an entertainment or a means of making quick money. If you regard them in this light then disaster is bound to follow your attempts to unravel their secrets. These ancient magical sigils do not give up their knowledge easily, as the shaman god Odin discovered as he hung on the World Tree Yggdrasil.

In occult workings the runes can be used, as all magical alphabets are, to add extra power to the ritual or spell. The act of having to carefully translate the ordinary letters of the alphabet into runes and the actual effort required to draw them concentrates the mind, which is the most magical tool we possess. Most of the runes can be translated directly into the Latin alphabet as follows:

F U D A R C X W H N I Z S

ᛏ ᛒ ᛟ ᛃ ᛈ ᛗ ᛖ ᛚ ᛟ ᛈ ᚱ
T B - - P E M L O - -

Before using the runes for magical purposes you should invoke the protection and guidance of Odin. A suggested invocation is given below, but readers can improvise their own as required.

Odin, Allfather, Lord of Shamans,
Possessor of arcane wisdom,
Lord of the Faery Hosts,
Wild Hunter of the midwinter sky,
Ruler of the Underworld,
Traveller at the crossroads,
I [*insert own name*] invoke and
call upon thee to aid me in the
Great Work.
At this time I seek [*state intention*]
with your help and through the
wisdom of the runes.
Lord Odin, grant me your
assistance.

During this invocation visualize Odin standing before you. His physical description is given in Chapter One.

The Magical Symbolism of the Runes

There are several ways in which the runic alphabet can be used for magic. One way is to use a single rune or combine several to make a magical charm. The uses of each character in rune magic are given below for easy reference.

For attracting wealth and protecting property.

To clear obstacles and change circumstances.

For protection and defence.

To increase communicative skills, pass exams and gain wisdom.

To ensure a safe journey.

To restore self-confidence and strengthen will-power.

To create harmony in personal relationships.

To bring happiness and spiritual transformation.

To attract positive influences.

To achieve long-term goals or help lost causes.

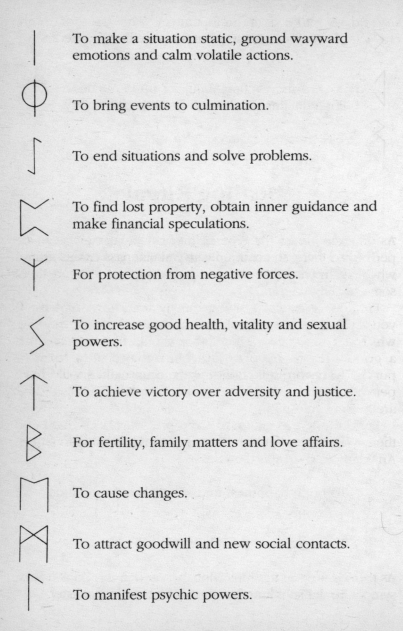

To make a situation static, ground wayward emotions and calm volatile actions.

To bring events to culmination.

To end situations and solve problems.

To find lost property, obtain inner guidance and make financial speculations.

For protection from negative forces.

To increase good health, vitality and sexual powers.

To achieve victory over adversity and justice.

For fertility, family matters and love affairs.

To cause changes.

To attract goodwill and new social contacts.

To manifest psychic powers.

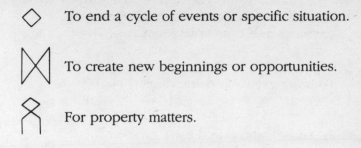

◇ To end a cycle of events or specific situation.

⋈ To create new beginnings or opportunities.

ᛉ For property matters.

Healing Ritual

As an example of the type of magical ritual which can be performed using the runes, let us imagine you have a friend who is ill in hospital and you have decided to send them some healing energy.

Prepare yourself by sitting quietly for a few minutes. If you have one, wear a robe or alternatively loose clothing which is comfortable. The clothes should be clean and it is a good idea to have a bath beforehand as a form of purification before commencing the ritual. You should have pen and paper to hand and a blue or white candle. (These are healing colours.)

Perform the invocation to Odin previously described and then write the patient's name on the paper in runic letters. An example is given below.

S A L L Y   B O W L E S

As there is no Y in the runic alphabet used in this book a solar symbol can be substituted as shown for the missing letter.

Below the name write the title and location of the hospital in runes as indicated below.

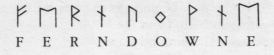

F E R N D O W N E

H O S P I T A L

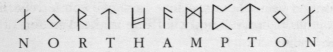

N O R T H A M P T O N

Then a petition to Odin, who as the Norse version of Mercury is a god of healing, and Baldur, who represents the life-giving rays of the summer sun is written in runes. A suggested wording for this is given below:

Mighty Odin, Lord of the North Wind
Baldur, shining light bringer
Beloved of the Gods,
I [*insert own name*] ask for the
power of healing to be sent to
Sally Bowles at Ferndowne Hospital,
Northampton,

I ask that she may be cured of
[*insert health condition here*]
and restored to good health
and full vitality.

I ask this boon not for myself
but on her behalf,
that the will of the Gods be done
and the laws of the Norns respected.

By the powers of wind and fire,
By the powers of earth and water,
By the holy names of Odin, Baldur,
Freyja and Thor, I ask it be done.

So mote it be.

The petition is read out in a strong, clear voice. The paper it
is written on is then burnt to ashes in the flame of the
candle. As you do so visualize rays of healing blue light
streaming out from the candle flame in the direction of the
patient.

As the paper burns the magician may visualize a ray of
blue light emanating from the forehead just above the bridge
of the nose, which is the site of the psychic Third Eye and
the physical pineal gland, towards the magical image of
Odin which has been materialized earlier in the ritual.

When this has been achieved, the magician thanks Odin
and Baldur for their help. Again a suggested wording is
given below:

I [*insert own name*],
thank thee Odin, grim lord of the dead
and guardian of the runes,
I [*insert own name*],
thank thee bright Baldur,
youngest of the North Gods.
Before ye depart to thy icy realms
beyond the Northern Lights,
I offer ye this sacrifice,

freely given, without pain or death
to any living creature.

A symbolic gesture of personal sacrifice is then made. This could be the burning of a piece of hair, a drop of blood drawn from the forefinger of the left (pagan) hand or the pouring of a libation of mead or wine.

As soon as this symbolic act has been performed, visualize the image of Odin slowly fading from view into nothingness. Before you start you may wish to consecrate the room you are working in. You can do this by imagining a circle of blue light surrounding it. This symbolic barrier prevents the ritual being disturbed by outside or negative influences. If required this circle of protection can be reinforced by evoking the elemental guardians of the north, south, east and west. Details of such evocations are given in my previous book *Candle Burning: Its Occult Significance* (The Aquarian Press, Wellingborough, 1975).

As an added (magical) bonus the healing ritual detailed above should be performed on a Wednesday (Woden's day) which is sacred to the god Odin. If possible the moon should be waning i.e. decreasing towards the new moon. Many occultists have an aversion to working magic when the moon is in the waning phase. This is a rather short-sighted viewpoint for on a waning moontide unwanted influences and illnesses can be effectively banished. When you should traditionally *never* work magic or indulge in occult activities of a practical nature is the period of three days before the new moon known as 'the dark of the moon'. In old folklore this time was allegedly ruled by the vampire goddess Lilith who attacked men sexually and was the queen of hobgoblins, ghosts and demons. She is of course the dark aspect of the Great Mother Goddess of prehistoric times who has always been feared by the followers of the patriarchal religions.

The Powers of the Gods

Different Nordic gods and goddesses can be invoked in rune magic for different purposes. Some of these are listed below together with their sacred days and planetary influences.

God/Goddess	Day	Planet	Rulership
Odin	Wednesday	Mercury	Healing, wisdom and knowledge
Freyja	Monday	Moon	Intuition, clairvoyance and psychism
Tiw	Tuesday	Mars	Courage and strength
Thor	Thursday	Jupiter	Wealth and material prosperity
Frigg	Friday	Venus	Love, fertility and childbirth
The Norns	Saturday	Saturn	Fate, destiny and luck
Baldur	Sunday	Sun	Healing, self-confidence and family

Descriptions of these deities for visualization purposes can usually be found in any good reference book from the public library on Norse mythology.

Norse Months and Festivals

As well as the days of the week the old Norse people had different names for the months than the ones we use today, which are based on Roman usage introduced when Britain was conquered by Julius Caesar and his legions. The Norse month names and the major sacred festivals are as follows:

Norse	Roman	Festival	Date
Wolfmoon	December	Night of the Mothers	21st
		Twelfth Night	31st
Snowmoon	January	Blessing of the Plough	1st
Horning	February	Festival of the Family	14th
Lenting	March	Summer Finding (Equinox)	21st
Ostara	April		
Merrymoon	May	May Day	1st
Fallow	June	Midsummer	21st
Harvest	August	Harvest Festival	28th
Shedding	September	Winter Finding (Equinox)	21st
Hunting	October		
Fogmoon	November	Heroes Day	11th

Amulets and Talismans

As well as using runes for invocations as a magical alphabet they can also be engraved on amulets and talismans. These can easily be worn as items of personal jewellery without fear of comment. An amulet is used to ward off negative influences and dispel bad luck. The talisman on the other hand is used like a magical magnet to attract good influences and positive vibrations to the person who wears it. Under normal circumstances a talisman is consecrated by its maker so that it attracts a specific influence, be it love, good health or money.

In Icelandic pagan magic special runic symbols have been created as talismans to attract various virtues for the benefit of the user. Iceland is still a very pagan country (it was not converted to the Christian religion until the eleventh century CE) and these runic charms are very popular. They are even openly on sale in the tourist shop at Reykjavik Airport from where the examples given below originate.

This is a charm used to grant wishes of all kinds.

This charm is used to ward off negative forces and protect the wearer from his or her enemies.

This sigil is used to prevent a rival magician from placing an evil spell on you.

Love charm. If worn around the neck on a silver chain this is said to attract the love of the person you most desire.

This is a charm used by Icelanders to attract money and prosperity.

Dress symbol. Write this rune sigil on a piece of paper or engrave it on a twig of birch wood. Place it under your pillow. Your dreams will come true.

This is not the old German Nazi swastika. It is the ancient Nordic magical symbol known as the Hammer of Thor. It is worn by pagan Icelanders who require the divine protection of the thunder god.

A runic cross which may be a Christian innovation for it protects the wearer from ghosts, evil spirits, demons and the faery folk.

The symbol above was widely used by Scandinavian sailors to prevent their ships being sunk in storms. Note the interesting similarity between this runic seal and the design of an anchor.

This last rune can be used to heal all sicknesses of mind, body and spirit. It is dedicated to Odin.

Magical Rings

Another potent use of the runes was on magical rings. In ancient tales of sorcery these rings were said to be able to make the magus invisible, protect him from evil or let him fly like a bird. Several rune rings have been discovered in recent years.

One, found at a place with the evocative name of Greymoor Hill, boasted thirty runes engraved on its surface. Twenty-seven outside and three powerful ones inside. Another rune ring found at Bramhan also had thirty runes, divided into three groups: nine, nine and twelve. These are lunar numbers and are associated with the phases of the moon, the Great Mother Goddess and the pagan Old Religion.

Magical rune rings have survived into modern times. One of the leading members of a German magical fraternity in the early twentieth century made a lucrative living by selling bronze rings inscribed with magical incantations written in the runic alphabet. He claimed the rings could protect their owners from illness and even sold them to German troops who were fighting in the trenches of France during the First World War.

CHAPTER SEVEN

CASTING RUNES

Today many people frequently consult astrologers, palmists, clairvoyants and mediums in an attempt to discover what is going to happen in the future. New Age shops sell Tarot cards, crystals and divining pendulums while thousands flock to psychic fayres which are organized all over the country. At a popular level, women's magazines and the daily newspapers publish sun sign horoscopes which are avidly read by millions of people. Futurologists, who use scientific methods to predict coming events, also earn high fees from corporations and governments who want to know about emerging social trends. The desire to know what the future will be is a powerful human instinct which has existed for many thousands of years.

To meet this demand for precognitive information there exists the art of divination, or the predicting of the future, by the use of psychic powers and occult symbols. Divination arose in ancient times and it is an art which is almost as old as humanity. Divination was an integral part of the shamanic tradition which, as we have seen, runs as a magico-spiritual thread through runecraft. The ability to be able to look into the future was regarded as a special gift from the gods to the shaman who in turn passed his or her knowledge on to the tribe.

One can easily imagine that in a society where the ability to survive from day to day was largely governed by intuition a person capable of predicting the unpredictable was much in demand. As tribal society became more sophisticated and complex, divination took on the form of a social science and gained a political dimension. Eventually it was integrated into the authoritarian state priesthoods which gradually replaced the shamans as the intermediries between the ordinary person and the spirit world. Even then the seer remained an important person in society and an advisor to the ruling class. In this way the diviner had a role which preceded the employment of professional future watchers in our modern society.

Shamanic Techniques

The training of a seer for divination was a long and arduous process which often took many years to complete. It involved periods of hard work under the guidance and control of an experienced initiated shaman, who had already served his or her apprenticeship. Novices in the psychic arts were initially taught self-discipline as an essential training for successful prediction. They were instructed in the mysteries of Nature including tuition in weather lore. At the end of this probation period the would-be seer could divine portents from the changing shape of storm clouds, the hunting cry of owls and the images reflected in a pool of water.

The shamanic training for seership also involved such well-known occult techniques as fasting, abstaining from sexual activity and sleep for short periods of time and many hours of meditation and trance. Only by enduring such physical hardships could the apprentice release the psychic energies within their bodies and achieve the necessary level of self-illumination which opens up contact with the spirit world. There were, of course, alternative methods used by some of the shamans to achieve this extra-sensory awareness more quickly. These methods included deep trance, ritual drumming and sacred dances. Natural psychedelic drugs such as the red-capped 'sacred mushroom' or fly agaric were also used.

The Sacred Mushroom

According to the ancient spiritual beliefs of the Eskimo shamans, the strange powers of the sacred mushroom to open the gates to the Otherworld were given to humanity by the Gods. It is related that the god known as Big Raven caught a whale while on a hunting trip. Raven was unable to send it back to his house under the sea because he could not lift the travelling bag containing all the provisions the whale needed for the journey. The raven god therefore called upon the Great Spirit to help him in the task. The Spirit told Raven, 'Go to flat place near the sea. There you will find the white stalks with spotted caps. They are the spirits who will help you.' Raven obeyed the instructions of the Great Spirit and went to the place indicated. The Spirit spat on the earth and where the saliva fell mushrooms sprouted. Raven ate the strange fungi and he immediately had the strength to lift the travelling bag so the whale could be taken home.

During the ritual act of eating fly agaric, the shaman will often see and communicate with the spirits of the mushroom. They materialize in a shape which resembles the actual fungi. The spirits are squat, with a brownish white skin which has a leathery texture. They have domed heads, wrinkled faces and long thin arms with spindly fingers which reach down to the ground. Their spirit bodies do not possess legs and they are rooted in the earth. Sometimes the mushroom spirits will ask the shaman to show homage by giving them offerings of food. Alternatively the spirits tell the shaman to worship the moon, trees, rivers and the hills. In every case, providing the correct rituals are performed, the mushroom people will permit the seer to see visions of the spirit world and look into the future.

This ritual use of the sacred mushroom within a religious or magical framework has to be clearly separated from the use of illegal social drugs or the consumption of legally addictive substances such as caffeine, alcohol, nicotine and medically prescribed tranquillizers in our modern society. While there is a considerable volume of evidence derived from both historical and contemporary sources to prove that the sacred mushroom can open up the psychic centres of the body, it is not a method the author would recommend. Without expert supervision, guidance and correct preparation the indiscriminate use of any natural psychedelic substance can have dangerous side-effects and should be avoided. Having made that point clear, the historical use of the sacred mushroom was well known in ancient shamanic cultures, including those of the Celts and the Norse people, where it was used in a ritual context by shamans with many years training.

Runic Divination

Whether or not the magic mushroom was eaten by the

seer prior to the event, the most common form of divination practised in pre-Christian Europe was the interpretation of omens from a bundle of arrows or sticks thrown down on the ground. The shape of the future was then predicted according to the pattern the sticks formed on the ground. The Chinese divinatory system known as the *I Ching* is probably one of the oldest and purest forms of this type of predictive art. In many ways the runes are similar to the *I Ching* but combine a pattern on the ground with mystical symbols.

One of the earliest references to runic divination is to be found in the writings of the Roman historian and traveller Tacitus who made a detailed study of the Germanic tribes and their magical practices. Describing the use of the runes, he says:

> They lop a branch from a fruit tree and cut it into strips, marking them with distinctive signs. Then they scatter the pieces at random on a white cloth. An official priest (if it is a matter of tribal importance) or the head of the household (if it is a private matter) prays to the Gods and, looking up into the sky, picks up the sticks one at a time and interprets them in accordance with the signs stamped on them.

The method used in rune divination has changed very little in the 2,000 years since this account was written. Individual rune casters, of course, use different methods for casting and interpreting. Some of these may differ in a few respects from others you may read about in the available literature on the subject, but the basic techniques are always the same.

Today there are many different sets of runes and even runic cards which are available commercially from shops and mail order services specializing in occult supplies. The quality of these differs considerably and the rune sets range from economically-priced plastic 'rune stones' to very expensive runic symbols made of gold or silver which may be worn as jewellery. For those who are used to handling Tarot cards, a pack of runic cards which illustrate each rune symbol may be more suitable then an actual set of runes.

Although you can buy your runes ready-made from an occult supplier or New Age shop it is a worthwhile and interesting exercise to attempt to make your own. This has several obvious advantages from a magical viewpoint. In actually manufacturing the runes you are exercising your own creative energy and permeating the runes with some of your life force. This creates a very powerful link between the rune set and the user which cannot be achieved by buying or using runes made by another person.

The traditional material for making runes is, of course, wood. Oak, ash and yew are regarded as the sacred woods which are best for rune making. Winter storms often mean that Odin has provided us with a plentiful supply of all these native woods. The oak has always been regarded in folklore as the King of the Trees and in ancient times was worshipped by both the Celts and the Saxons. It was the sacred tree of the Aryan thunder/sky god who in Norse mythology was represented by Thor. The ash is a tree whose name is derived from the Old Norse *aska* meaning 'man' and it is said that Odin created the first human being from an ash tree. An ash (or the yew) was also said to the cosmic World Tree Yggdrasil. The yew, as we have seen earlier, was the tree of death and the Otherworld. It is sacred to Odin as the shaman god and Lord of the Wild Hunt.

The shape of the runes is a matter of personal choice. They can be square or oblong with rounded corners for easy handling. Alternatively they can be circular, oval or elongated with round edges at each end. With regard to the size of the runes, they should be small enough to be able to fit into your hands for casting. Round runes should be approximately 1"-1½" in diameter while oblong or square runes can be 2"-2½" in length. Larger sizes tend to get a little bit cumbersome to handle.

When making wooden runes the actual symbols can be painted or carved on the surface. Some rune makers burn the characters into the wood and then paint them afterwards. This produces quite an effective finish. The traditional colours for runes are either royal blue or purple for Odin, red for Tiw symbolizing male energy and the life force, or green for Freyja representing Nature and fertility.

If you plan to gather the wood for the runes from its natural setting be environment friendly and if at all possible use fallen branches. If you really have to cut a new branch, ask permission from the tree spirit first and then leave a small offering of a coin or an alcoholic libation as a sacrificial token afterwards. If you are going to buy your wood from a DIY store or timber merchant's, ensure it is virginal and do not haggle over the price.

When not in use the rune set can be kept in a small pouch with a drawstring. This bag can be made of cloth, velvet or leather. Although I have not come across a knitted rune bag it is an interesting idea! Tacitus mentioned that the German shamans used a white cloth on which they cast the runes. This is an optional extra for the modern runecaster but is used by many practitioners.

Before using the runes for the first time they should be consecrated or blessed in a simple ritual. This is performed by lighting a blue and a green candle and sprinkling salted water over the runes. This should be spring water or (unpolluted) water from a stream. As you do so the following simple blessing can be recited:

Odin, Master of the Runes,
Freyja, Mistress of the Runes,

Bless and consecrate the runes
which I [*insert name*] have made,
Ensure that the guidance I give
with them will be right and
correct,
Grant me thy wisdom and insight
to see what lies ahead.

The meanings of the runes in divination are linked to their magico-spiritual symbolism in the northern European pagan tradition. A comprehensive guide to their predictive symbolism is given below. In use the runes can have either a mundane or spiritual meaning. It is the runecaster who has to decide at what level they are going to interpret the reading or a specific rune. For some people a spiritual meaning may be more relevant while others, in this particular incarnation, may not be working on themselves spiritually. In such cases the more mundane meaning is more appropriate. Often, however, a mixture of both can be offered as in any situation, personal relationship or problem the spiritual and material aspects cannot be separated. The old shamans and rune wizards were well aware of this fact and for this reason the runes are a very practical system to work with. They deal both with the realities of everyday life and the spiritual realm beyond it.

Prediction Symbolism

FEOH   Upright: Money, success, great wealth.
          Reversed: Bankruptcy, loss of personal
                    esteem, failure.

The emphasis in any interpretation of the Feoh rune is

financial attainment. When the rune appears in a reading in its positive, upright position there is a clear indication of money moving towards the querent. This could be a salary increase, a small win on a game of chance or a cash gift from another person who is close to the enquirer.

The position of this rune in relation to others in the cast should be checked very carefully for further clues. If it falls near a love rune like Gyfu or Beorc then the source of the money would be connected with a personal relationship or even marriage. Associated with Rad, financial increases could be the result of a business trip or short journey. Near Odal, the money might be from a legacy or will.

If Feoh turns up reversed in a reading then it is a warning not to fritter away resources on personal whims or lost causes without any thought for future security. If that path is followed financial disaster is bound to be the end result and will lie ahead for the querent. Personal reserves should be consolidated and a budget plan put into action to prevent any wastage from monetary sources.

Feoh warns us not to be too materialistic in our general outlook on the world. In the Eighties the pursuit of wealth by the yuppy culture resulted in a social climate where greed and envy were rampant. Too much money can be just as much a burden as too little. There is absolutely no spiritual virtue in poverty but gross materialism can be just as soul destroying.

Money which is in excess to personal requirements should be shared with the less fortunate and, as my magical teacher wisely told me, 'Money is made round to go round.' The cosmic law says that whatever you give out will (eventually) return to you threefold. This law of cause and effect, of course, covers both positive and negative things. The stockbroker in his Porsche who drives past the homeless in their cardboard boxes should learn the lesson offered by the Feoh rune.

Spiritually, this rune instructs us that the hidden treasures of spirit should not be coveted by a priestly elite but, wherever feasible, given out to those who seek them. In the past spiritual truths have been obscured in mysterious mumbo-jumbo or preserved within a corrupt religious power structure to which ordinary people had no access. With the coming transition to the new Aquarian Age these outmoded practices are destined to pass away. However, the initiate of the Mysteries should beware of selling spirituality in the market place and be discriminate in their choice of student.

The esoteric meaning of Feoh is that the enquirer should not hide their spiritual light from the outside world. With caution, they should endeavour to share their gifts (healing, psychic insight, occult wisdom etc.) with those who seek their guidance with an open mind and without prejudice.

⊓	*UR*	Upright:	Good fortune, advancement in career, robust health.
		Reversed:	Missed chances, negative influences, bad luck or minor illnesses.

The auroch or wild ox in Northern European history and myth was a symbol of male sexual energy. It represented strength, stamina and virility and therefore upright in a rune reading Ur indicates the querent, of either gender, will experience a period of good health and boundless energy. If the enquirer happens to be a man, the powerful aspects of this rune's influence in his life will be increased.

However, this is also very much a rune of challenge. As the Norse youths had to fight and subdue the wild auroch in order to take their rightful place in society so the Ur rune signifies the commencement of a phase where life will throw up numerous challenges for the querent. This is not necessarily a negative development unless the rune is reversed, for we all have to learn the lessons offered by the school of life and there are no free lunches.

Therefore when Ur appears in a reading the enquirer should be prepared for some changes in his lifestyle and some exciting events ahead. If the rune is nicely upright, these will be beneficial changes in career prospects or a general transformation of life for the better. Change is the one constant law in the universe and we resist it at our peril.

This leads us to the reversed meaning of the Ur rune. Sometimes we are faced with the opportunity of change and we either resist it or, fearful of the unknown, turn away from the challenge it offers. This attitude is indicative of the faint-hearted warrior who flees in panic from the charging auroch and loses his chance of a position of influence within the tribe.

Reversed, this rune can also highlight any negative thoughts possessed by the enquirer which are preventing him from progressing in life. On a physical level the rune is a pointer to minor health difficulties which may limit the individual's choice of action or affect his ability to achieve lasting success. For the male querent this could be a lack of self-confidence or even sexual impotence.

On a spiritual level the Ur rune has to do with will-power and the more elementary forces inherent in the human psyche. The latter have to be controlled, or sometimes sublimated, if the enquirer plans to step on to the spiritual path. Sublimation however should not be confused with repression and these forces can be rechannelled into creative powers without completely stifling their natural energy.

In a rune reading where spiritual matters are being examined or discussed, Ur can represent a person who has rejected a totally hedonistic lifestyle and become aware of non-physical levels of existence. The querent has chosen to assert his or her individuality in a spiritual way and is ready to face the challenges offered by the Wyrd.

PORN	Upright:	Protection, an important decision, good news from afar, unexpected luck.
	Reversed:	Beware making any hasty decisions, bad news.

In contrast to the powerful animal symbolized by Ur, this rune is represented by the tiny thorn. However this is a deceptive symbolism, for the thorn was also a metaphor for Thor's mighty hammer Mjollnir which he used to right wrongs and defend the weak. The keyword when Porn appears in a runic reading is therefore 'protection' and it can be taken as a sign that the querent is blessed by the gods and is being guided in his or her actions by the force of justice.

The rune also suggests an important decision is to be made shortly. This decision will be crucial to the enquirer's well-being in the future. Porn indicates that it might be very prudent to obtain a second opinion in this matter rather than going it alone. If this is done information will be forthcoming which will enable the querent to make the right choice or will indicate whether or not the decision should even be taken. Providing the right course is followed, all will be well in the end.

If in a reversed position, the Porn rune warns that extreme caution should be taken in making any decisions or changes in life. The need to take expert advice before proceeding is underlined, for failure to do so could lead to complications and an unfortunate result. The old adage, 'Fools rush in where the Gods fear to tread', is very apt when Porn is reversed in a reading. It is a prediction of a time when it is far better to sit back and do nothing then be precipitated by events into taking the wrong path.

Spiritually and magically this rune is one of the most powerful and should always be treated with the respect due to Thor. As a protective charm it can be used to ward off negative forces (symbolized by the frost giants in Nordic mythology) and protect the innocent from harm. When the enquirer is actively working on a magical or spiritual level, Porn is a rune representing the small discomforts in life which have to be endured. By themselves these discomforts, like thorns, are merely irritating, but with the heightened awareness which is a by-product of the spiritual path, they can assume monstrous proportions which are not comparable to their real size.

These minor tests of character are all part of the learning process and have to be accepted. If the seeker is not capable of ignoring or rising above those petty distractions of daily life then he or she is not ready to meet the more important, and substantial, challenges offered by the spiritual quest. If the going is already becoming too hard then the querent should re-evaluate his life goals and decide if he really wants to pursue a path of spiritual responsibility in this incarnation.

	OS	Upright:	Wisdom or wise counsel from an elderly or knowledgable person, communication and learning.
		Reversed:	An elderly person who causes problems, incorrect advice from a spiteful source, rumours and lies.

The two key words associated with Os are 'wisdom' and 'communication', for this is the rune sacred to the shaman

111

god Odin. If this rune is found in a prominent position in a reading it may mean the querent is an intellectual type, a scholar, a person interested in communicating ideas or a seeker of wisdom. He or she could be a teacher, a journalist, an advertising executive or an occultist.

Odin was regarded by the Romans as the Norse equivalent of Mercury or Hermes. While we generally imagine Odin as the archetypal old man or shaman, this rune can also represent the influence in the enquirer's life of a youthful person bursting with ideas and possessed of good communicative skills. It can also indicate the beginning of an apprenticeship or period of training during which the querent acquires extra skills, knowledge or experience which enhances his natural talents.

Interpreted on the other level using the old man archetype, Os can suggest that the querent will receive wise advice from an older person or someone who is in a position of authority or influence. As Odin is known to wear many disguises when he walks the highways and byways of Middle Earth this encounter may be unexpected. There could even be an element of intrigue or mystery surrounding it. However, it could also be a meeting with someone as mundane as a bank manager, words of wisdom from a parent or an interview with an employer. If Beorc is close to this rune in the reading it could even be the enquirer's mother who offers the advice.

When reversed Os is a strong indication that some mischief is afoot. The person seeking guidance should be advised by the runecaster to guard against confidence tricksters, smooth talkers or anyone offering 'get rich quick' schemes. It is an omen of a confused atmosphere which makes separating fact from fiction very difficult. It is a time when lies and rumours are the order of the day and nothing is as it first seems. During this muddled phase the querent must keep alert and watchful for Odin has a cunning side.

He is often economical with the truth and cannot be always trusted.

The spiritual significance of Os is connected with the oral transmission of esoteric knowledge. In ancient Scandinavia the shamans of both sexes were renowned as skilled practitioners of the bardic art, which was used to convey spiritual teachings to the masses and among the initiates of the pagan Mysteries. Sacred songs, poetry and *galdr* or magical incantations all played a role in runecraft. The Os rune teaches the seeker that wisdom often originates from unexpected sources, even the mouths of fools and babies. The seeker should never be surprised at the guises used by Odin to reveal his presence in the material world.

R	*RAD*	Upright:	Travel, a journey away from home, a holiday which brings joy and enhances life.
		Reversed:	A bad or difficult journey, delays, a visit to sick relatives or friends in trouble.

As we have already seen, this rune is linked with the symbolism of wheels and wagons and thereby to movement or journeys. Usually this element of travel is to do with pleasure and could therefore be a holiday or a short trip away from the home environment like a weekend break. It could also be a visit to see friends or even a business journey.

The actual nature of the journey is in itself unimportant, for the key factor is that any type of travel broadens the mind and opens up new horizons. While we may think we are just going on a pleasant holiday or a day out to the coast to relax and enjoy ourselves, the chance to see different places and encounter new people will subtly alter our perception of life. The experience, however mundane it may appear, is part of the soul's learning process which is the reason why we incarnated in a physical body.

Sometimes the querent may find himself in circumstances where a lesson has to be learnt the hard way. This likelihood is indicated by Rad appearing reversed. Often we have to make personal sacrifices and make a journey which before we even set off we know will be arduous and unpleasant. However, it still has to be experienced, and it is better to face the prospect positively than with a gloomy or pessimistic attitude. It is, after all, part of our personal growth and we can gain insights from the unpleasant as well as the nice things life has to offer. Delays are also possible and when this rune is in a reversed position the enquirer can expect to miss travel connections, lose items in the post or get lost on journeys. The advice offered by the runecaster should be that all important journeys should be postponed until conditions improve.

For the spiritual seeker Rad warns that it is shortsighted to take the soft option or the easy route, even though it is naturally far easier to sit and wait for the teacher to ring your front-door bell rather than making any effort yourself. In our modern society instant enlightenment is often promised, but seldom delivered, by the gurus of mass market spirituality. They may promise the earth but the truth is that the gates of heaven are harder to open than they may suggest.

The message of the Rad rune is that the querent who is seeking spiritual illumination must be ready to make the effort to travel in search of new experiences. This does not mean picking up your backpack and heading off for India. However, in the northern European tradition the shaman often went off alone into the forest to isolate himself from the outside world. These short journeys of self-discovery were regarded as an important aspect of the shaman's training and were used to recharge his psychic batteries. For most of the time the shaman lived and worked among the ordinary people participating in the wheel of death and rebirth but sometimes he needed this period of isolation for self-reflection.

This rune therefore teaches the spiritual aspirant that he cannot afford to become isolated from the day-to-day events which make up the fabric of existence. Life is the great initiation and the spiritual quest is the greatest journey we can ever embark on. Sitting behind your lace curtains and watching the world pass by while waiting for a spiritual teacher to appear is not the way of the true seeker.

<   *CEN*   Upright: Spiritual enlightenment, artistic creativity, guidance from divine sources.

                                  Reversed: Loss of prestige, social standing and material possessions.

The rune of Cen symbolizes the elemental power of fire. In Norse mythology fire was regarded as one of the primal cosmic energies which brought the universe into manifestation. This rune is a representation of the masculine aspect of the creative life force which permeates physical existence. When it appears in a rune reading it is an indication of fiery energy working the querent's life and surroundings. This can manifest as an increase in physical well-being or, if the enquirer possesses these abilities, the overwhelming urge to be creative in the artistic field.

Cen also offers openings to forge new relationships or bring a fresh burst of energy to existing ones. If things have been stagnant for a long time, this rune burns away the dross and allows change to occur. The Cen rune is a sure sign that change is on the way and that old problems will be swept away by a new flow of energetic action. It can also promise sexual activity if the querent has been leading a celibate life. This is especially emphasized when Cen appears next to Tyr or Beorc in the cast.

When this rune is reversed or inverted (facing left instead of right or upside down) its meaning is explained by the word 'loss'. This could be personal belongings, like jewellery or a wallet, or heavy expenses incurred through over-indulgence in the luxuries of life. Generally, if reversed, it indicates a restrictive period when limitations are placed on the enquirer in a material sense. It can also be a sign that a long-standing relationship is about to reach its final point as the fires of passion and the heat of commitment have faded away.

Fire has been a spiritual symbol for enlightenment or illumination since ancient times. In pre-Christian days, sacred fires were lit on the hilltops at the vernal equinox to encourage the return of the sun, which was regarded by many pagan peoples as a heavenly symbol of the masculine life force. The initiate who has achieved spiritual enlightenment is often said to be 'inflamed with spirit'.

In the Old English poem which gives the symbolic meanings of the runes Cen is associated with 'the torch of living flame' which 'burns most where noble folk are settled within'. This is a reference to the Indo-European aristocratic class, who were often initiates of the pagan mysteries, and to the royal dynasty who where priests and priestesses of the Old Religion. The 'noble folk' could also be an euphemism for the spirits of the dead. In a rune reading interpreted on a spiritual level, Cen can signify the receipt of guidance from sources beyond the physical realm.

X	*GYFU*	Upright: A gift which is a symbol of shared love and binds together a relationship.

The giving of gifts is a very important and significant gesture in human bonding. There is an old saying that money cannot buy love or happiness. Unfortunately in modern Western society marriage is often a business contract. It therefore has very little to do with romantic or spiritual love but is based on financial security underpinned by sexual attraction. It has to be remembered that all too often money can be used as a weapon of control and domination.

If interpreted on a mundane level, Gyfu suggests the enquirer is soon to be given the opportunity, should he or she desire it, of changing a temporary relationship into one which has a more permanent basis. This may be marriage in the conventional sense or an event which will lead to an increase in the emotional intensity or material circumstances of a relationship, such as the commitment to live together.

Gyfu can also indicate that the 'gift' is in fact a totally new relationship which is unexpected. Because of the nature of this rune, this love affair will be a happy one and could lead to a degree of permanence at some future date.

When this rune is looked at spiritually it reverts to its ancient meaning of a sacrifice to the gods. This act always has repercussions and when a gift of this type was offered it had to be repaid in some way. The sacrificial offering is a contract between the celebrant and the divine forces he or she is invoking. Once the worshipper had dedicated themselves to the gods the terms of this contract applied.

As Odin sacrificed himself on the cosmic tree to gain the wisdom of the runes, so the seeker must understand that there is a price to pay for acquiring occult knowledge. It is not as dramatic as the sacrifice that Odin made but sometimes the price to be paid is the emotional happiness represented by the rune of Gyfu.

ᚹ   *WYN*   Upright: Joy and happiness, the transforming of life for the better.
   Reversed: Unhappiness, grief, loss of affection.

The Wyn rune offers a positive image when it is presented upright in a reading. It is a portent of good times ahead and a set of personal circumstances which produces a large degree of happiness and joyful events. It is possible the querent has been experiencing a difficult period but this rune is a harbinger of good news. Things are moving once again and a new cycle is beginning which will transform life for the better.

Unfortunately, if Wyn is reversed the opposite is true. Life is beset by problems, difficulties and hindrances which seem unsurmountable. The enquirer may feel depressed and be lacking in confidence. It is possible he may be feeling restricted in an employment situation or in relationships and have the urge to break away. Because depression is often projected onto those around us, the querent may feel that his or her loved ones do not care about his predicament or do not understand these claustrophobic feelings. It has to be impressed on the enquirer that these feelings are a temporary phase and will eventually pass away.

In a magical sense Wyn is said to be the rune that makes the deepest wish come true. This however can be a double-edged benefit as sometimes what we think we want is not always what we need and even the brightest dream can turn sour. On a spiritual level, this rune is the realization of the eternal human desire for the perfect society or utopia where happiness is everyone's birthright. It can also symbolize the romanticized view of the spiritual path which many neophytes suffer from until their eyes are opened to its true realities. In some ways Wyn is a rune of magical glamour and it can cast its aura of enchantment on to even the most down-to-earth, rational person.

When we look around at the world and its problems it is sometimes very difficult to be joyful. Famine in Africa, the environmental crisis and the general inhumanity of humanity to its fellow beings offer a bleak vision of the future with things gradually getting worse. Wyn does offer the promise that nothing is permanent and change for the better is always a possibility around the next corner.

Pessimism and depression are negative emotions which can be fundamentally destructive for those suffering from them and anyone they contact. Often we inflict unhappiness on ourselves by adopting the wrong attitudes of gloom and doom. It has to be accepted that we incarnate here to learn through experience. Once this simple fact is registered and accepted at a conscious level we can learn to adopt a more positive reaction to the stresses of daily life.

HAGEL	Upright:	A delay in plans which are not ready.
	Reversed:	Disasters caused by natural forces, delays created by circumstances beyond human control.

As we saw earlier, this is the rune which is representative of the destructive forces of Nature that sometimes disrupt life without warning. You may be sitting comfortably in front of your television set when a sudden storm rips the roof off your house. This is the force symbolized by the Hagel rune which causes a sudden change in well-laid plans.

In a reading Hagel predicts unexpected delays or the postponement of plans, especially those made some time ago. While this may seem to be a negative happening at the time it is possible that a good reason for the delay will become apparent at a later date. This rune therefore has a hidden side which is best expressed in the old cliché that every cloud has a silver lining – even in a hail storm!

When this rune is reversed, then the enquirer should be told to be very cautious when executing long-term plans. The cosmic conditions are definitely not right for ambitious moves and if the querent decides to ignore this advice and proceed then disaster will follow. It has to be accepted that there is a time for everything. When the disruptive forces of Hagel are working the wise person keeps a low profile and waits for circumstances to improve before proceeding. Combined with a reversed Is or Nyd rune the adverse effects of Hagel are increased considerably and it may be time for the enquirer to take out extra insurance.

When the spiritual path is being walked it can often feel as if you are being swept along by forces beyond your control. This can be a very unsettling feeling when it is first experienced as we all like to think we are the masters (or mistresses) of our own destiny. As the ancient shaman learnt to divine the omens from weather lore, so the seeker will eventually understand the ways of the Wyrd. He or she can learn to flow with the forces of destiny rather than fight against them in a futile struggle for supremacy. Understanding the way the cosmos and its laws operate is essential to the education of the seeker in the spiritual ways. Once this is achieved, the seeker becomes aware of the divine pattern behind life and the role they play in it.

ᛉ	NYD	Upright:	The forces of destiny are working, caution is needed, resist greed.
		Reversed:	Hasty action leads to failure, be inactive or proceed with care.

Patience, it is said, is a virtue but in the hustle and bustle of everyday life it is difficult to cultivate. As with the previous rune, this shows the tendency to take quick action is rash and leads to disaster. Unless you are aware of the workings of the Wyrd and the role they play in life then valuable time and energy can be wasted. It has to be understood that the forces of destiny are playing their part in human affairs and what will be, will be, whatever course you take.

Nyd also advises against greed and the pursuit of material satisfaction at the expense of spiritual concerns and emotional happiness. Obviously we live in a modern world and it would be wrong to reject the physical comforts offered by technological progress. However we should clearly recognize the difference between desiring material objects which are superfluous to an acceptable way of life.

When reversed, the enquirer may be feeling the odds are stacked against him. It would be better to reconsider any action which is contemplated or even cancel it rather than proceed hastily and be defeated. If things are not going right there is a reason, and the querent should examine his or her motives carefully and correct anything which might be hindering the successful completion of the project in hand.

The Nyd rune is ruled by the Norns who administer the forces of Wyrd and control the web of life. In a spiritually-based reading this rune signifies the point where the seeker has become aware of both the material and the spiritual planes of existence and realizes they are complementary. He or she has realized that there is a spiritual dimension beyond the physical senses and has began to explore the Otherworld which is the magical domain of the shaman.

	IS	Upright:	The end of activity, cooling of a relationship, disagreements with close friends.

This is another rune like Hagel which signifies delays in the progression of activities undertaken by the querent. Ice is a static substance, so Is can be seen as an indication that matters will be frozen where they are or placed in cold storage until a later date.

The symbolism of the Is rune suggests the enquirer may want to keep the matter on ice for some time until enthusiasm returns and the matter can be reactivated. As with Hagel, the enquirer should sit tight and wait for better conditions rather than proceeding with the plans they have.

On an emotional level this rune is not a good omen. When related to a love affair it is a sign that there will be a 'cooling off' period. Those involved need time apart to decide what they want from the relationship. It is unfortunate that once the heat of passion has gone cold it is often difficult to rekindle the flame of desire or interest.

When read spiritually, it is an important rune. Is represents one of the twin primal energies which created the universe from chaos. Ice is an energy form which by its very nature attempts to resist the law of change. The conflict between ice and fire creates the opposing, yet strangely complementary, polarities which enable the universe to manifest on the physical plane. As water freezes into ice so Is represents the cosmic process by which spirit becomes matter.

In Judaeo-Christian mythology the opposite forces of light and darkness, male and female, matter and spirit, good and evil, etc., are seen in purely dualistic terms. This had led to the idea that there is an eternal struggle going on between opposing forces in the universe as if in a cosmic chess game. Mastery of the universe is the prize to be given to the eventual winner of this spiritual struggle. This concept is directly contradicted by pagan philosophy which sees the polarities as complementary energies capable of blending together in the union of the opposites.

⌀	*GER*	Upright:	A warning not to judge, others or you will be judged, harsh words may end a friendship, end of a cycle.

When the Ger rune is prominent in a reading it is a reminder that natural justice is a powerful force which none of us can escape. 'As we sow so shall we reap' and every action we make has its corresponding reaction. At harvest time we gather in the rewards from seeds planted earlier in the year. How we have sown those seeds and tended the young plants will determine the type of harvest we can expect for our labours. If combined with the Is rune, Ger signifies karmic retribution for past misdeeds.

The spiritual meaning of Ger is the end of a cycle and the beginning of a different one which takes the seeker a stage forward in the quest. The keyword of this rune is the natural justice found in Nature which is eternal. It has to be understood that cosmic law is eternal and has little relevance to the transitory legal standards imposed by human social groups. Ger teaches us that everything, like the cycle of the seasons, moves in circles and that our linear concept of the progression of time is an illusion.

⌐	*EOH*	Upright:	Death, news of a friend or enemy from the past, the recurrence of old problems, false nostalgia for the past.

Many people are frightened of Eoh because it is often called the death rune. It *can* mean this in a reading, but also refers to news received by the querent from someone he or she has lost contact with. This person could either be a friend or someone opposed to the enquirer's best interests. Considering the nature of this rune it could even be a spirit message from someone who is deceased.

It is also a prediction that old problems the querent thought had been solved will return to haunt him from the past. This is because they were not dealt with effectively the first time around and there is some clearing up of old energies to be done before the matter is finally resolved. Also, while it is good to have fond memories of past events we must not dwell on the glories of yesteryear or conjure up mythical 'good old days' that did not exist but move on into the present and the future. As L. P. Hartley once said, the past is a foreign country, and they do things differently there.

When a reading is being scrutinized for signs of spirituality, the Eoh rune offers the seeker the teaching that death is not something to be feared but another step in the evolution of the soul. While there is no written evidence for reincarnation as a popular belief among those who used the runes in ancient times, it did play an important part in many pagan religious systems. The reality of reincarnation was symbolized in the ancient myth of the sacrificial death of the pagan gods and their rebirth as enlightened beings. This can be seen in the stories relating to the sacrificed gods such as Osiris, Adonis, Tammuz and Odin.

PEORTH Upright: Hidden knowledge, unexpected gains from a mysterious source or a secret gift, a spiritual guide.

Reversed: A secret from the past is revealed which causes harm.

As the divinatory meanings show above, the Peorth rune is connected with these things which are hidden or concealed from view. It can represent money or gifts which come to the querent without prior warning. If found near the Nyd rune, it is the paying off of karmic debts.

When reversed or inverted, Peorth is a negative rune and warns that old skeletons kept safely locked in the closet will be discovered and made public. Past scandals or indiscretions which the enquirer thought were well concealed or forgotten will be made known to the outside world. This rune knows where all the bodies are buried.

When the rune is considered spiritually, a different energy altogether is at work. The querent has reached the point where help will be offered by another person. Peorth indicates this person will act as a spiritual guide and will point the way forward along the path. It would be nice to think that Odin himself will materialize to help the seeker personally. This is always possible, but it is more likely that this guide will be a little more difficult to recognize. As the jester's mask often hides the face of a wise man, so the seeker could find it difficult to discover the true nature of his or her guide. Real adepts seldom wear cloaks and pointed hats covered with stars so that you can recognize them in a crowd.

| EOLH | Upright: | The banishment of negative influences, a new career or friendship. |
| | Reversed: | Danger, material loss, misleading people. |

This rune tells the querent that he or she should look out for the possibility of a new career move which will be lucrative. An offer will be made which the enquirer will find difficult to refuse, and if he accepts it will affect his personal circumstances very beneficially. In general this rune is a sign of an expansive stage in life when the sky might just be the limit.

An alternative meaning for Eolh is 'friendship'. When the rune features in a reading the querent should expect a new friend to arrive on the scene. This new friendship will be a very positive event and probably long-lasting. It might be with a person of the opposite sex and be platonic. However, if Tyr or Beorc are nearby, look out for romantic strings attached.

If reversed, Eolh offers a psychic warning of danger emanating from a subtle source. The querent should be on his guard and keep his wits sharpened for an attack from any direction. People he knows to be unreliable or dishonest should be avoided, or if they have to be dealt with, treated with suspicion. This is also a time when material losses could occur due to theft, unwise investment or carelessness about personal security.

When Eolh is read on the spiritual level it represents the temptations the seeker will come across on the path which attempt to divert him or her from the straight and narrow. Often it is hard for the spiritual person to reconcile their ordinary life with the demands of the inner life and this can lead to conflict and distress.

Sometimes the seeker will encounter people who will try to sidetrack him from the path into areas which are outside, or contradict, the spiritual life. With any form of magical energy there is always the temptation to use it for selfish and sometimes anti-social purposes and this must be resisted. Eolh is foremost a protection rune and symbolizes the deflection of negative energy which enables the seeker to find his or her true path to spiritual enlightenment.

SIGIL   Upright: Health, wise direction.

When Sigil is found in an isolated position in a reading the runecaster can be confident that the person seeking advice has few health worries. However, for accuracy it should be read in relation to the other runes near it. For instance, if it is to be found near Hagel, Nyd or Beorc (especially if these runes are reversed) there could be some health problems lurking around the corner.

There is a warning here against over-exertion, bad diet, the dangers of executive stress and generally 'living on the nerves'. If this is allowed to continue over a period of time it could lead to a loss of physical vitality and the depletion of the body's natural reserves of life force. If the querent gets into this position, the weakened immune system comes under attack and illness can develop.

Spiritually, this rune is a symbol of the higher self which directs the personality of the incarnated soul along its Wyrd path in this life. The sun is both a symbol of consciousness and represents the natural cycle of birth, growth and death. This cycle can be found in the turning of the seasons and the life of a human being from youth to maturity and then old age.

Sigil teaches the seeker that they are following the spiritual path because that is their mission in this incarnation. While the higher self and soul remain detached, the lower self incarnates in a physical vehicle in order to experience through the personality chosen for this particular lifetime. While most people remain blissfully unaware of the existence of the higher self, the spiritually-developed person knows that their life is being guided and there is a plan to it mapped out at birth yet with the added ingredient of free will.

↑ *TYR*	Upright:	A sexual relationship, emotional fulfilment, success with legal matters.
	Reversed:	Unrequited love, marital problems, litigation.

This rune is in the form of a phallic shape and so it is pretty obvious what its meaning will relate to. It indicates the masculine trait of intellectual firmness which can be found in both sexes. Unfortunately this firm purpose can degenerate all too easily into a narrow-minded outlook or 'tunnel vision'. Male energy is individualistic and can often ignore or ride roughshod over the concerns and sensibilities of the group. Tyr also represents the mechanics of the law, and justice can sometimes be blind.

When this rune is cast in a reading for a male querent it usually represents himself and the runes near it are therefore very significant. If the enquirer is female then Tyr symbolizes her closest male relationship, whether it be father, brother, friend, lover or husband. Tyr usually signifies a sexual relationship, and the nature of this, and its possible outcome, can be divined by examining the runes that fall closest to this one.

When reversed, the sexual aspects of Tyr take on an opposite interpretation. The rune could mean the end of an existing emotionally-based relationship, a period of celibacy, a frustrated and one-sided love interest or problems arising in a long-standing partnership. When Tyr is reversed and the querent is male it indicates he may not be happy with his masculine image or is feeling inadequate or threatened emotionally at a physical level. This is a common male problem. When the enquirer is female, a reversed Tyr suggests she is having trouble with men in general. These problems might stem from emotional difficulties or negative experiences in the past which she has not overcome.

When examined spiritually, the Tyr rune indicates courage and tenacity as motivating forces driving the seeker on along the spiritual path towards his goal. It is the way of the spiritual warrior who defends the cosmic laws in the name of universal justice. The Viking *berserkers* and the medieval code of chivalry, which involved a knight dedicating himself to a noble lady (representing the Goddess) and fighting evil, is exemplified by the positive male energy of the Tyr rune.

BEORC   Upright: New beginnings, birth, marriage.

Beorc is often called the fertility rune and can mean either a birth or a wedding. This symbolism can be taken quite literally or, if circumstances do not allow this, it could be the birth of a brainchild or the start of a new venture. The wedding could merely be the union of two minds with a common objective. Analysis of the runes surrounding Beorc will show the outcome of these events on either level.

When this rune is cast in a reading for a female enquirer it usually represents herself. If the querent is male, it is his closest female relationship. This could be a mother, sister, friend, lover or wife depending upon his personal circumstances.

In a spiritual interpretation of Beorc, the Anglo-Saxon poem which describes the meaning of each of the runes states that while the birch has no fruit it is still a beautiful tree. This rune warns the seeker not to be misled by physical appearance. In myths and fairy tales the old hag may be a princess in disguise and the ugly frog can be transformed into a hunky prince by a kiss.

The Beorc rune also instructs the spiritual seeker not to disregard the erotic delights of the 'pleasures of the flesh'. The pagan path is not an ascetic route to spiritual enlightenment and does not deny the physical body or its functions. In pre-Christian religious practices the sex act was regarded as a divine sacrament in the worship of the life force. The early Church, with its tradition of puritanism, was horrified by this idea and condemned the element of eroticism in pagan ritual, which they falsely regarded as evidence of 'devil worship'. However, the sexual aspect of spirituality was not regarded by the pagans as a licence for rampant permissiveness, as we shall see when we examine the next rune.

M *EH* Upright: Travel, house removal, job changes.
　　Reversed: Restlessness, travel difficulties.

The archetypal energy which controls Eh is based on movement, so therefore the key words used to interpret it are 'travel' and 'physical relocation'. If it happens to fall close to Rad there is every indication of new employment which will involve either travelling or moving home. Combined with Beorc it suggests family consultations will be required before a decision is made. Near either Rad or Lagu gives an indicator as to whether the travel element involves a short or long distance.

Reversed, Eh is a sure sign that the enquirer is becoming restless in his or her present environment. This could be work or home life and the querent is either frustrated by the 9 to 5 routine or feeling claustrophobic about his physical surroundings in general. Again, the divining of adjacent runes will provide extra information enabling the runecaster to point a way forward that will resolve these twitchy feelings. In a reversed position there is also a warning that a journey soon to be undertaken will be time-consuming and the querent will feel at the end of it that he might as well have stayed at home.

As we saw earlier, the magico-spiritual meaning of Eh is related to horses and specifically the mystical steeds rode by the shamans to reach the Otherworld. While the Beorc rune teaches us not to reject sexuality, even on the spiritual path, Eh issues a word of caution in this area. It tells us that physical desires should not be allowed to become an obsession and rule our lives. In this respect sexual magic involves techniques of containment as well as liberation. The life force is a powerful energy which must be controlled and channelled. If this is done then beneficial results can be achieved from the use of sexual energy in the magical arts.

MANNAZ Upright: Relatives, contacts with the outside world.
Reversed: Self-imposed isolation, trouble from enemies.

When casting the runes Mannaz is symbolic of the querent's interaction with his or her kindred and humanity as a whole. When positively placed, it offers the prospect of co-operation and team work which will lift a burden from the enquirer's shoulders. Willing hands appear from nowhere and what seemed like a difficult problem will be resolved through the application of the talents of several other people. It also foretells that any contacts the querent makes outside his or her immediate environment will be important ones that enlarge the querent's perspective and increase the range of experiences he has previously had.

If reversed, however, Mannaz predicts that within a short period of time the enquirer may feel isolated from the outside world and cut off from contact with those he or she usually relates with. This isolated position may be one which is deliberately chosen by the querent. He may want to sort out personal problems and reflect on his next move. It can also mean that help will not be forthcoming from those around the querent and the US Cavalry cannot be seen coming over the hill. If this rune is close to Hagel or Nyd it could even be that negative influences, possibly created by the querent, will be an obstacle blocking the way ahead.

131

Spiritually, Mannaz relates to the connection between humanity, the microcosm and the world or universe, the macrocosm. The esoteric teaching of 'as above, so below' indicates that we are made in the image of the gods and are therefore part of the universe we inhabit. In poetic terms, 'no man is an island', and the holistic vision of the Aquarian Age which depicts the human race as passengers on Spaceship Earth with all her other life forms is relevant here.

On a personal level, this rune is a sign that the seeker may, however reluctantly, be forced to cut the umbilical cord from their family once they start to seriously tread the path of spiritual awareness. Often those on the path feel that the scales have fallen from their eyes and they see the world in a totally different light. They may feel distanced from their family and existing circle of friends for this reason. New relationships must be forged but when this is not possible, and fellow seekers cannot be found, then it has to be accepted that the spiritual path can sometimes be a lonely experience.

	LAGU	Upright:	A journey across water, inspiration, intuition.
		Reversed:	Confusion, delusion, muddled thinking.

The initial meaning of Lagu is a trip across water. Obviously this may be a journey abroad. However if the enquirer has a river near his home then a shorter journey is indicated.

Lagu is fundamentally a feminine rune which is often said to be ruled by the moon. It is associated with the releasing of psychic power, the use of intuition as a problem-solving tool, and creative inspiration. The latter will usually be of an artistic or poetic type. Magically, concentration on this rune can increase psychic abilities, inspire creativity and can be used to heal health problems relating to menstruation and the female reproductive organs.

In a reversed position, Lagu's positive benefits evaporate in a mist of confused thoughts, wrong decisions, muddled actions and deluded ideas about yourself and others. It can be a sign of a lack of creative energy and the very unpleasant condition known as 'writer's block' which is the curse of authors. Whether the enquirer is male or female, this rune predicts contact with a neurotic woman whose influence will be disruptive. A male querent might become romantically involved with this woman with disastrous results, while his female counterpart could have her private life undermined by the newcomer's tiresome meddling.

Spiritually read, Lagu may indicate a period of self-doubt when the seeker wonders if the hardships of the quest are really worth the effort. Like a land dweller not used to travelling on the sea, he or she may feel that they are drifting aimlessly and that the shore is receding in the distance. This condition is sometimes known as 'the dark night of the soul' and is a common experience among those who have deliberately decided to change their lives on the spiritual level. It has to be accepted and will eventually pass as the seeker realizes that they now possess the reserves of inner strength needed to overcome self-doubt.

◇   *ING*   Upright: News of a stranger, realization of a dream.

The overall meaning of the Ing rune is 'completion'. It signifies the end of a phase of activity and the start of a new one. Usually this is a successful conclusion to a matter in hand and the person involved finds themselves free to pursue other directions. In many ways it is a liberating experience, for the querent can move on knowing that he or she has achieved something worthwhile and there are no loose ends which need tidying up. If Ing is found close to the Beorc rune in a reading it can be taken as confirmation of the safe delivery of a baby.

When the runecaster finds Ing in a reading which is interpreted on a higher level, it is a sign that the enquirer has reached a state of inner harmoney and feels at-one with himself and the world. Whether this exalted state is permanent or merely transitory, only time will tell. We all experience this type of feeling during life, but few people can exist in this blissful state for long periods of time while incarnated on the material plane. However the Ing rune tells us that the union of the opposites, the cosmic forces of fire and ice, within the psyche is the goal of the spiritual quest.

 DAEG   Upright: Prosperity, a new dawn
                                    leading to a far better life.

The symbolism of this rune is emphasized by the key word 'dawn'. As the start of another day brings new experiences so the Daeg rune is a good omen offering the chance of a fresh beginning and the promise of better times ahead. It is a very optimistic and positive rune to have in a reading. Study of the runes around it will show the nature of what is to come in the future. If there are any reversed runes in its vicinity then Daeg will soften their impact on the general reading.

Daeg informs the spiritual person that he or she must seek beyond duality for the true reality and meaning of life. Darkness has traditionally been labelled as the (evil) opposite of light by the monotheistic, patriarchal religions which replaced paganism. In pre-Christian religion, however, light and darkness are recognized as complementary opposites, for one cannot exist without the other. The dawn always follows the night.

An understanding of this truth will lead the seeker to a new vision of the universe and their role in it. Light and darkness are balanced energies without whose interplay the cosmos would not exist. Daeg symbolizes the point where these forces are polarized and synthesized at the same time to create reality.

 ODAL Upright: Property, legacies.
      Reversed: Legal problems with land or property.

This evaluation of the runes began with Feoh, which signifies the wealth represented by cattle in ancient society. With Odal we have come full circle, as this rune deals with the property and the possessions acquired with that wealth. Specifically it covers all matters dealing with property (the ancestral home) but also pension funds, stock and shares and inherited possessions or money.

When reversed, Odal indicates losses in the above financial areas or a serious legal problem relating to money matters or perhaps the changing of a will. If this rune turns up reversed the querent should watch out for a tax inspector looking for undeclared earnings. It can also show that the enquirer is someone who thinks money grows on trees and is in for a rude awakening leading to material loss. It can also signify a miser who is obsessed with making money at the expense of normal human relationships. This is especially true if a reversed Feoh rune is near to Odal.

Spiritually, this is the rune which tells the seeker that he or she has reached the culmination of a particular stage in his journey or self-discovery. The quest, of course, never ends until the soul is freed from the wheel of death and rebirth and, like a larvae turning into a butterfly, is trans-cended to another state of existence. This process can take countless incarnations to achieve.

Odal, above all the other runes we have described, reflects the fact that the journey embarked on by the seeker must eventually lead back to where he or she started. As the wise sage told his disciple, 'The further one travels, the less one knows.' However, the valuable lessons learnt on the quest may be of use to the seeker in this life or, like inherited possessions or property, can be passed on to illuminate a future incarnation.

Reading Runes

It has to be remembered that it took the ancient rune wizards many years to learn the inner meanings of the individual runes and master their various interpretations when combined with the other runic characters. Frequent practice and plenty of experience are needed if you wish to follow the craft of a runecaster. This has to be combined with a sincere desire to help other people with their prob-lems and a deep understanding of human psychology.

Having learnt the rune meanings, how do you physically cast the runes for divination? If a rune bag or pouch is being utilized, the runes can be shaken and the querent is asked to select a number of runes at random from the container. The number taken will depend upon the type of reading required, as we shall see later.

In an alternative method, the runes can be shuffled in the bag and then actually cast on to a flat surface or the rune cloth. Those runes which land face upwards are read and the others are disregarded. Another technique is to lay all of the runes face downwards on the rune cloth and then move them around so they are well mixed. The querent is then asked to choose the desired number and these are placed face upwards.

Invoking the Guardians

Before casting the runes it is recommended that you invoke the traditional guardians of the runic alphabet, the Nordic gods Odin and Freyja. A suggested invocation is given below but you can use your own wording as desired.

Great Odin, Master of the Runes,
Wise Freyja, Mistress of Hidden
Knowledge
Guide my hands and thoughts
that my questions be
answered, true and right,
by the power of fire, earth,
air and water.
So mote it be.

Rune Casting

There are several different runic lay-outs and methods of reading which can be used to answer a variety of questions. Several are given on the following page.

One of the simplest spreads is the triple rune reading which is very effective for answering a single question on a specific matter. In this cast three runes are selected using one of the methods described above. They are placed side by side as indicated on the following page.

The triple rune reading will provide a concise answer to the question or problem facing the querent and the runecaster may not need to do a general reading involving all the runes.

An alternative to this, where a shorter reading is required, is known popularly as the Cross of Thor. In this type of reading four runes are cast or selected. They are then placed in the form of an equal-armed cross of the elements which is an ancient pagan symbol. A fifth rune is then chosen and placed in the centre space of the cross.

Moving deosil, or clockwise, around the cross from the base, the runes are read as follows:

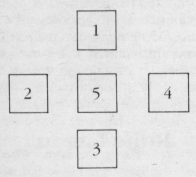

Rune one represents the general nature of the influences surrounding the enquiry. The second rune on the left-hand side of Thor's Cross represents any obstacles which are facing the querent in relation to the problem or the question. Rune three at the top of the cross illustrates the type of forces working in favour of the querent. Rune four on the right-hand side of the cross is the short-term or possibly immediate consequences to the enquirer of the answer to the question. Finally, the fifth rune in the centre predicts the long-term outcome of the reading in the querent's life.

The Runic Wheel

This is a more complex form of reading which can provide a generalized forecast of the major trends and changes in the querent's life over a 12-month period. The bag of runes should be mixed up and then 13 runes are selected from the bag one at a time. These are placed on the casting cloth using a circular pattern in the shape of a wheel. Commencing at the nine o'clock position and working deosil around the imaginary circle 12 runes are placed in position as if on a clock face. The final rune or indicator is placed in the centre of the wheel. It symbolizes the overall influence or guiding force which permeates the reading.

It is recommended that the runes are placed face downwards and only revealed in turn as the caster moves around the circle until the wheel is completed exposed. Runes next to each other or on opposite sides of the wheel can be linked and further analysed at the end of the reading.

Each of the positions on the Runic Wheel rules a specific area or sphere of influence in life as follows:

First: Health matters; the self; energy and male sexuality.
Second: Material possessions; money and personal security; female sexuality.
Third: Relatives; communication; short visits; friendships; media matters.
Fourth: Home life; the immediate environment; domestic matters.

Fifth: Creativity; sports; gambling; financial speculation.

Sixth: Relationship with outside world; community affairs; social contacts.

Seventh: Partnerships; the opposite sex; marriage.

Eighth: Religion; legacies; the forces of law and order.

Ninth: Travel; legal matters; philosophy; education; publishing.

Tenth: Career; social status; family matters.

Eleventh: Personal interests and hobbies; distant friendships.

Twelfth: Secret life; private fantasies; escapism; service to others.

Becoming a Runecaster

The runes are ancient symbols rooted in myth and magic which represent powerful archetypal energies which exist in the universe. They are not New Age toys or psychological tools, although their use will open up the personality and allow access to hidden parts of the psyche. When practising divination, the runecaster is using the runic sigils as a focusing point. They enable him or her to tune into the energies they represent. To a lesser or greater extent all of us are psychic but often this gift is submerged through social conditioning, adverse environmental situations or simply our own inability to accept the reality of an existence beyond the physical realm which we can see, touch and feel. Some people are naturally sensitive and have no difficulty in establishing contact with the Unseen. This type of person makes an ideal runecaster and ideally should be able to also read the portents from other divinatory systems such as the *I Ching* and the Tarot.

A few words of advice are needed for the would-be

runecaster. First of all if you decide that you want to take on the responsibility of predicting the future, then you must learn to respect the confidences of anyone who consults you. Generally people come to a diviner when they are in trouble and will ask advice relating to the most intimate areas of their life. Naturally anything they tell you should not be passed on to a third party without their prior permission or in extreme circumstances only. In common with doctors, priests and lawyers, the diviner is bound by a moral obligation of confidentiality.

When dealing with emotional problems, the runecaster should avoid introducing a moralizing tone into their interpretation of the reading. Whatever the private views of the diviner on such sensitive social issues as adultery, incest, divorce, abortion, drug addiction or homosexuality, it is essential the runes are read in a detached, unbiased way and that any advice which is offered is not coloured by personal prejudice. It is ethically wrong for any diviner to use a reading as a cover for dictating a course of action based upon their own personal beliefs or opinions. The enquirer can be given advice, but the final interpretation of the reading must lie ultimately in their hands only.

Finally, it should be noted that the interpretations given in this book are based on the traditional meanings of the runes derived from historical sources and modernized accordingly for the present age. However, they are not dogma and it is possible that as you learn to work with the runes variations on these meanings will become apparent to you. In this way new insights into the richness of the runic alphabet as a divination tool can be revealed and hopefully shared with others following the art of runecraft.

May the Old Gods bless you in your work.

FURTHER INFORMATION

Readers can obtain further information about the pagan Old Religion and runecraft by contacting the following publications and groups. Enclose a sae for reply.

The Cauldron
Caemorgan Cottage
Caemorgan Road
Cardigan
Dyfed SA43 1QU

Runestaff
142 Pheasant Rise
Bar Hill
Cambridge

English Odinist Hof
BCM Tercel
London WC1N 3XX

The Odinic Rite
BCM Runic
London WC1N 3XX

The Runic Guild
BM As Wynn
London WC1N 3XX

Odinn
36 Dawes House
Orb Street
London SE17 IRE

INDEX